# IGNATIUS LOYOLA

## SPIRITUAL EXERCISES

**THE CROSSROAD SPIRITUAL LEGACY SERIES**
Edited by John Farina

*The Rule of Benedict: Insights for the Ages*
by Joan Chittister, O.S.B.

*Ignatius Loyola: Spiritual Exercises*
by Joseph A. Tetlow, S.J.

*Francis de Sales:* Introduction to the Devout Life
*and* Treatise on the Love of God
by Wendy M. Wright

*Teresa of Avila: Mystical Writings*
by Tessa Bielecki

*St. Francis of Assisi: Writings for a Gospel Life*
by Regis J. Armstrong, O.F.M. Cap.

*Augustine: Essential Writings*
by Benedict J. Groeschel, C.S.R.

*Thomas Aquinas: Spiritual Master*
by Robert Barron

*Hildegard: Prophet of the Cosmic Christ*
by Renate Craine

*Karl Rahner: Mystic of Everyday Life*
by Harvey D. Egan

*C.S. Lewis: Spirituality for Mere Christians*
by William Griffin

*Anselm: The Joy of Faith*
by William Shannon

*Dante Alighieri:* Divine Comedy, *Divine Spirituality*
by Robert Royal

*John of the Cross: Doctor of Light and Love*
by Kieran Kavanaugh, O.C.D.

# IGNATIUS LOYOLA

## SPIRITUAL EXERCISES

═══ ✛ ═══

*Joseph A. Tetlow, S.J.*

CROSSROAD · NEW YORK

This printing: 1999

The Crossroad Publishing Company
370 Lexington Avenue, New York, NY 10017

Copyright © 1992 by Joseph A. Tetlow, S.J.

Printed in the United States of America

---

**Library of Congress Cataloging-in-Publication Data**

Tetlow, Joseph A.
    Ignatius Loyola : spiritual exercises / Joseph A. Tetlow.
        p. cm. — (The Crossroad spiritual legacy series)
    ISBN 0-8245-2500-0
    1. Ignatius, of Loyola, Saint, 1491-1556. Exercitia spiritualia.
    2. Spiritual exercises. I. Title. II. Series.
    BX2179.L8T44 1992
    248.3—dc20                            92-20692
                                                  CIP

# Contents

## INTRODUCTION

## FIRST WEEK

98510

# Foreword

Writing in the fourth century a North African Christian by the name of Lactantius offered the following definition of virtue. For him, virtue is nothing less than "enduring of evils and labors." How unlike contemporary notions this definition of virtue is and how odd it sounds for us to be told so plainly that the fulness of life can be had only through enduring evils and trials. Yet, despite our inclination to write off Lactantius as an overly pessimistic nay-sayer, we must admit that life does include a large dose of suffering. We can take it well or badly. We can flee it or embrace it, but it will come and find us wherever we hide, and then it will test our mettle. Virtue does involve suffering evils, not simply actualizing ourselves, or conquering our fears, or visualizing success, or learning techniques to cope with stress, or building better "relationships" with members of the opposite sex. There are things in life that simply cannot be so easily manipulated. Situations that don't get better. Unpleasant realities that won't go away. Where do we turn when confronted by them?

We can turn to the externals, to our comforts and our conveniences, to the superficialities of our lives, or we can turn to our depths. Many who have lived before us have learned the hard way that turning to the depths is the way to a fuller life. Their insights have been handed down, often in forms that are now hard to find and harder to read. Their language is archaic. Their morality out of sync with ours. Their clarity, offputting. Their humility, disconcerting. Yet they are there, waiting quietly to share with us their hard-won wisdom, waiting to dialog with us as we face situations that are different from those they encountered only in the particulars, not in the essences.

Simply put, that is the reason why Crossroad, myself, and a team of well-known scholars and spiritual leaders have joined together to undertake the Spiritual Legacy series. The need for spiritual wisdom is great. Our situation is critical. This then is more than an enterprise in scholarship, more than a literary exercise. It is an effort to convey life.

Certainly the idea of doing editions of the works of spiritual guides from the past is not new. There are a host of books available that do just that. How is the Spiritual Legacy series different?

The uniqueness of this series abides in its content and its style. In content it endeavors to present both texts from the spiritual guide and extensive commentary by a present-day disciple of the sage. It gives the reader the chance to encounter for herself the writings of a spiritual master. Nothing can take the place of that experience. However demanding it might be, whatever efforts it might require, there can be no substitute for it. One, for instance, cannot simply hear a description of the tenth chapter of Augustine's *Confessions.* No commentary, however skilled, can take the place of reading for oneself Augustine's words of unparalleled power: "Late have I loved Thee, O Beauty, so ancient, yet so new!"

While it is true that there is no substitute for encountering the text first hand, it is also certain that for most people that encounter will be an excursion into a foreign land. Often many centuries and numerous barriers of language, customs, philosophy, and style separate us from the writings of bygone sages. To come to that point where we can understand the horizon of the author, we must be taught something about the historical context, the literary style, and the thought forms of the age, for instance. That is why we have included in this series extensive commentary on the text. That commentary is alternated with the text throughout the books, so that one can be taught, then experience the writings first hand, over and over as one moves deeper into the text. At that point, the horizon of the reader meets that of the author, aided by the expert guidance of the editor of each book, who suggests not only what the text might mean, but how it might be made part of our lives.

The style of the Spiritual Legacy series is also unique in that it attempts to convey life with a certain degree of sophistication that befits an educated readership. Yet it does not assume that everyone will have a background in the material presented, nor does it purport to offer original or arcane scholarship. The editors' mastery of the texts is in each case complemented by their experience in putting the meaning of the texts into practice and helping others to do so as well. We are trying to present a series of books that will fit somewhere between the scholarly editions that pride themselves on their accuracy and originality and the popular pieces that offer too little substance for the healthy reader.

The series is designed to be used by a broad range of people. For those seekers who wish to journey toward spiritual wholeness as part of a group, the series is ideally suited. The texts presented can be easily divided into sections for discussion by a group meeting, say, on a weekly basis.

For those who are traveling alone, the series is a trustworthy and enjoyable tour book. The direct, simple language of the commentaries frame the memorable words of the classical texts and offer them in an attractive setting for meditation and practical application.

The publisher and editors of the Spiritual Legacy series join me in inviting you to undertake a journey that will take you back to an encounter with ancient wisdom and challenge you to an experience of self-understanding and, at its best, self-transcendence. It is our hope that that experience will help you to grow and to be a source of fresh life for all those around you.

*John Farina*

# Preface

The six Jesuits who were murdered in El Salvador in 1989 were men whose scholarship flourished in the public forum, who were deeply committed to the people's total liberation, and who lived day to day under the threat of lethal violence.

They had been formed by St. Ignatius of Loyola's Spiritual Exercises. I hope that their spirituality informs this book, which I have thought of as homage to these Companions of Jesus.

What I have learned of Ignatius's Spiritual Exercises, I have learned from many men and women who have willingly let me hand on to them what had been willingly handed on to me. I owe most to the younger Jesuits whom I have accompanied through thirty-day retreats. Some of them have caught the fire and are passing it on, among them Brian F. Zinnamon, Vincent R. Malatesta, and Francis W. Huete.

Many of the insights in this study are rooted in the work of Canadian Jesuit Gilles Cusson and of American Jesuit George Ganss. The interpretations in it were honed in discourse with Dr. Eileen Raffaniello and Dr. Juan Lorenzo Hinojosa. The book could not have been written without the support of the Society of Jesus, given through Edward Arroyo; I am grateful to him and to my two fellow pilgrims, Jesuits John Padberg and Thomas Clancy.

The book was suggested to me, and the basic idea for its structure sketched out, by Dr. John Farina, general editor for the Crossroad series. Anyone who has worked with an excellent editor will know his value in making books and will understand my gratitude to him.

# Introduction

The *Spiritual Exercises* of Ignatius of Loyola took shape in his own religious experience and in the experiences of the women and men he helped. Ignatius made the book for himself to start with, to remember accurately what helped others to a deep and enduring experience of God in their lives. He basically created a handbook for his work as spiritual guide. He did not change this: in its final form, it presents both materials and intricate instructions for guiding another person through a structured, coherent experience of God.

Men and women have been going through these Spiritual Exercises for 450 years. At this time, more men and women are going through them and directing others through them than at any other time during their history. Moreover, whereas until a generation ago only thoroughly trained Jesuits directed people through the experience, now many women and men, religious and lay, have been trained and use the book skillfully and with good results.

What is there in Ignatius of Loyola's Spiritual Exercises that makes them as accessible a religious experience today as they were 450 years ago? Is the experience the same? What do people who make thirty-day retreats hope to accomplish? What actually happens?

To answer these questions, you need to know something about Ignatius and his religious roots in late medieval and early Renaissance spirituality. You need to know how the book developed out of his personal conversion to Christ within the church and out of his work over two decades to evangelize others and reform their lives. His work, however, continues; so you also need to know how women and men now experience the Spiritual Exercises.

## An Accessible Translation

This book attempts to address those questions by presenting both a fresh translation into modern English and a descriptive commentary on the past and present experience of the *Spiritual Exercises*.

The translation is not *literal* in the ordinary sense of that word, but what Jesuit scholar George Ganss calls "a functional equivalence." In point of fact, compared with other current translations, it moves further away from Latinisms and the inelegant sentence structures of Ignatius's Spanish and further into the idiom and structures of modern English. For this translation aims more at making readily available the basic sense of Ignatius's Spanish that interested readers expect and less at preserving the sacrosanct technical terminology that directors must know and master. The difference, however, is not an opposition, but a stress.

In making the translation, I used what scholars call the "autograph text," which they consider entirely authentic because, though it was made by a copyist, Ignatius corrected it and added to it in his own hand. The definitive edition of this text, along with the three most important Latin translations, was published by José Calveras, S.J., and Cándido de Dalmases, S.J., *Sancti Ignatii de Loyola Exercitia Spiritualia*, Monumenta Historica Societatis Iesu, vol. 100 (Rome: Historical Institute of the Society of Jesus, 1969).

In any such translation, the matter of sexually inclusive language rises, which is important in this particular text. The *Spiritual Exercises* has been well translated into non-sexist language, serving a sound purpose. The changes required, however, exacted the price of not preserving a strong focus on the individual who is going through the Spiritual Exercises, the structured prayer experience the book guides. Inclusive expressions like "he or she" or "they" make the book sound as though Ignatius were talking about Everyperson. He is not; he was careful whom he invited into this experience and always mindful of that unique individual. That mindfulness must not be lost to inclusive language.

Furthermore, Ignatius is a masculine author and his spirituality begins in the masculine. His *Spiritual Exercises* are logically ordered, charged with vision and idealism, fixed in hierarchical authority, full of masculine images, and submit experience to abstract ratiocination. These are the more masculine traits. Carl Gustav

Jung noted this and wondered why Ignatius did not lean less on animus and more on anima.

The truth is that Ignatius did indeed rely on anima, which in him was fully developed, contrary to his current plaster-cast image as drily military. He fills his book with emotions and feelings, a large sense of harmony, intimacy, intense personal relations, tenderness, and a prime concern for each person's gifts and desires. These are the more feminine traits. They indicate, among other things, that Ignatius learned from the many women who befriended him and also from the ones (no small number) he guided through the Spiritual Exercises.

This dual source of energies makes it equally possible for women and men to go through and to direct others through the Exercises. In view of all this, in the translation I keep the singular pronoun and keep it masculine where Ignatius writes it masculine (which does not make his language sexually exclusive). I have chosen to use sexually inclusive language in the commentary.

## A Descriptive Commentary

A description of the experience of the Spiritual Exercises and a commentary on the spirituality they embody requires attention to the history and theology behind them and to current experience as well. It asks the fairly direct question, What is it like to go through the Exercises?

Ignatius elaborated his spirituality in a considerable number of documents, and an extraordinary number of his writings are extant and published. He wrote the *Constitutions of the Company of Jesus* (the Jesuits) and many brief essays and instructions. We have some of his personal records concerning the founding of the Company and his prayer, and "the pilgrim's story," a brief autobiographical narrative that he dictated in his last years. We also have about seven thousand letters. All of these, deriving from the Spiritual Exercises and reflecting that experience, give valuable help in interpreting that book.

I have therefore woven the history of the book and its basic spirituality into a narrative description of the experience. In the narrative, I tried to introduce experiences and materials at the points at which they commonly occur in the thirty-day retreat or in the Exercises done at home (formats explained presently). In a sense, I have tried to describe a typical experience of the Exercises, a fairly optimistic undertaking. The narrative depends on the stories of the first Companions of Ignatius of Loyola and of Jesuits through history. But even more than that, it reflects the experiences of the many men and women I have been privileged to accompany through the Exercises in all the ways of going through them.

## ✤ Comment 1 ✤

# The Author of *Spiritual Exercises*

Iñigo López de Loyola, the Basque *gentilhombre* who would become Ignatius of Loyola and the author of *Spiritual Exercises*, lived through a massive tide in human history. Within a year of his birth in 1491, Columbus reached the Western Hemisphere and marked the ripening of European exploration into colonization and worldwide trade. All of his life, Ignatius would hear of further horizons and yet further dreams of wealth and glory. One of his brothers signed the usual papers declaring himself dead (explorers usually died as explorers) and sailed to die in what is now Central America.

His own family had fought to drive the Moors from Spain, which *los Reyes Católicos* (the Catholic Kings) achieved the year after Iñigo's birth. All his life, his world was divided into two immovably hostile forces, Christianity and Islam. Shortly after Ignatius's death in 1556, the thousand-year-old flood of Islam into Christian Europe began to ebb with the Battle of Lepanto.

By the time Iñigo had reached the age of reason, the Iberian peninsula had come out of a century of political and economic chaos. The cities and towns had focused power, so that Iñigo's brother, head of a great estate, had a simple one-man vote in the local council that his father and grandfather had dominated. The great dynastic powers, like Ferdinand and Isabella's, had been established in much of Europe, making liegemen of the heads of families like Iñigo's and creating a class of courtiers. Iñigo was one of them. The dynasties warred incessantly, much as our world does, and Iñigo dreamed as a boy of heroic service as the king's loyal man.

He dreamed from the bottom. He was the youngest of seven sons and one of thirteen children. He was farmed out to a wet-nurse for rearing, and his mother died early on in his life. His father bequeathed him only instruction in Spanish and a blessing, so at age seven the Basque-speaking boy started learning Spanish. Helped by connections in his mother's family, he was sent to the court of the king's treasurer, Don Juan Velázquez de Cuéllar, whose memory he was to cherish the rest of his life.

Iñigo went as a venturesome scapegrace and took to court life wholeheartedly. He learned weapons and loved to use them, and he learned the poetry of courtly love and of Christian devotion. In his time, gentlemen listened carefully, spoke deliberately, kept the faith inviolate, and loved the Mother of God, Holy Mother the Church, and their own honor. Real men did not go much to church, but they believed fiercely and loved ardently. And they knew how to be friends and loyal companions, gifts that shone in Iñigo.

When his first protector fell into disgrace with the king and died, his lady saw to it that Iñigo had horse, weapons, and a bag-ful of gold. He had no trouble finding service under the Duque de Nájera, governor of his home ground. And he had no trouble con-tinuing, he would later say "out of force of habit," to gamble, carry on romantic affairs with women, brawl, and provoke swordplay on points of honor. He served the duke well in a couple of armed skirmishes in the unending wars between France and Spain, the only grounds for calling him a soldier. The truth is that Iñigo, really a courtier graced with great tact and comprehension, gave more valuable service as an arbitrator and peacemaker.

### The Fall at Pamplona

In was in the duke's service that he rode thundering into the lit-tle town of Pamplona in May of 1521. Once more, the French had moved south of the Pyrenees and once more the Spanish had countered. Iñigo galvanized the citadel to a frankly hopeless de-fense, impressing the French but not thwarting them. As he stood on the parapet directing the fight, a cannon ball the size of a big man's fist cut him down at the knees.

He was helped back to Loyola by the admiring French. The ensuing surgeries, once to reset his right knee and again, at his insistence, to saw off a protruding bone, were savage. Iñigo made no sound. In June he seemed about to die, but on the eve of St. Peter's feast took a turn for the better. Then he lay there week after week for seven months.

In his boredom, he turned from daydreaming romances to spiritual books offered him by his sister-in-law, now mistress of the house. Day by day, he lay reading Spanish translations of the century-old *Life of Christ* by Ludolph of Saxony and of the *Lives of the Saints*, written two centuries earlier by the Dominican Jacobus de Voragine. Ludolph calls Jesus Christ our "foundation," and Voragine pictures Christ in life-and-death battle with the Enemy, both of which Iñigo grasped at and wrote into his *Exercises*. Having learned from chivalric romances, he dreamed of heroic deeds, fame, and a splendid marriage. Now as he read about the ascetical and evangelical exploits of St. Dominic and St. Francis, he began dreaming different dreams. God seized him in the midst of this, one of the great conversions recorded in human history. Iñigo took copious notes in an exquisite hand as he learned to see himself and his life world differently: a different nobility, a different service, a different Lord.

He began keeping a record of what touched him, a practice he kept for the rest of his life to honor the gifts God lavished on him and to grow in spiritual maturity. He told a Companion that he had written three hundred sheets during these months; few doubt that he would later put some of that into the *Spiritual Exercises*. During these months, he had supernatural visions. One night, the Lady Mary appeared to him carrying the Child; from that experience came a steadiness in sexuality that never left him, and he remained profoundly and peacefully chaste.

He discovered Christ as his Lord and he identified sin as his defeat. He knew that he would have to live penitent for a time, perhaps living like Francis of Assisi. Then he began to hope to go to live and work in Jerusalem among the infidel. He kept all this to himself, partly to avoid family opposition (it came) and partly out of the reticence of the gentleman.

## The Pilgrim Begins

He left home in March of 1522, dressed properly and mounted like a gentleman, at his brother's insistence, but with his leg still in bandages. He went to the Duque de Nájera asking for his back pay, from which he paid debts and very possibly made some provision for women. Along with all the good points, Iñigo's culture condoned concubinage, and his ideal of courtly love furthered marital infidelity. He had left behind him in Loyola a priest-brother living with the mother of his three acknowledged children and his oldest living brother, head of the family, with a concubine who visited regularly. He had kept part of the money to pay for the repair of a shrine of the Mother of God, who was from now on the Lady of his life.

Now he felt himself free to make the pilgrimage to Jerusalem that he had determined on. To prepare for it, he went to the reformed Benedictine monastery at Montserrat. There he made a complete confession of his life, taking three days to finish, and told his confessor about his secret purpose of finding a new life in Jerusalem. After his confession and under cover of night, he stripped off his courtier's clothes and gave them to a beggar. Then, dressed in a pilgrim's rough gown and following proper courtly ways, Iñigo kept a night watch at the shrine of Our Lady. He stood and knelt through the vigil of the feast of the Annunciation, knee or no knee. In the morning, he left his sword there before his Lady and went down the mountain.

As the newly elected pope, Adrian of Utrecht, the last non-Italian until the present pope, traveled the same roads, Iñigo started toward Rome. He thought to spend a brief time of fasting and praying in a little town named Manresa, where he lodged first in the poor house and then with the Dominicans in a spare back room. His mindset was that of the armed courtier exploring savagely wild ground. He did what he thought he had to do. He began living like a beggar, eating as a vegetarian, and drinking no wine. A fastidious man, he chose to attack his vanity directly by leaving his fingernails filthy and his tawny hair in greasy tangles. His physical penances, which very likely included scourging himself and wearing sackcloth (townsfolk at first called him "the sack man"), damaged his health, and he would later on include in a little note in the *Spiritual Exercises* the advice he regularly gave against excess in penances. He visited monks and priests all the time. Weeks passed. He confessed weekly, conferred regularly, attended Mass daily, and prayed for seven hours in each twenty-four. He was to spend a year at Manresa while God taught him, in his own expression, "like a little schoolboy."

Winter softened and Iñigo's penitence matured in the spring toward love of God. He was daily at Mass, reading the Passion, and he doted on conversation about spiritual things with the learned and the unlearned both. The desiccate summer set in, and with it came a dryness and emptiness of spirit that puzzled Iñigo. It swirled into a mistral of self-doubt and scruple, a ferocious desert of temptation. His sins seemed ineradicable. He confessed them again and again, always finding some detail that could spell damnation but never finding any help. At the edge of sanity, he stood near an excavation and saw peace in its dark depths: suicide. He cried out to God in anguish, "Help me, Lord, for I find no relief in other people or in any creature." The once arrogant courtier vowed he would follow a puppy did it lead to peace.

He woke one day realizing that this way led from God, not to God. He judged that his confessor ought to have instructed him to stop raking through the past. He began grooming himself and eating meat, all the time keeping up his prayer. He also kept talking with people about God, at first because he enjoyed it and then because he saw that he was, in a stock phrase he used the rest of his life, "helping souls."

### The Illumination at the Cardoner

One day he walked along the town's little river, Cardoner, toward a roadside shrine. With no warning, he found himself stopped and immersed in God — not just his freedom, so that he yearned and loved, but his understanding, so that he knew and comprehended. He was given a deep sense of how all creatures emanate from God and, in Christ, return to God; how Jesus Christ completes human nature in taking our flesh; and how Christ is present in the Sacrament. He grasped that God's plan is really a project that each person on earth contributes to, and how what God hopes in us rises in our consciousness and, by God's grace, to free enactment.

Iñigo would later say that he learned more in this time than in all the rest of his life together and that he would offend God were he to deny the reality of any of it. In its afterglow, he shaped his spiritual conversations in the plaza and in people's homes more positively. At first he could not talk enough about the Blessed Trinity; but then he noted that he enjoyed this more than the people he was talking to did. So he grew bold enough to start talking with them on topics they needed to hear about: the waste of any sinful action, the names of our daily evildoing, the threat of living lost forever. An almost extravagantly systematic man, he noted down what helped them among lessons of his own spiritual experience (having no schooling in theology to draw on). Gradually, he had talked through the whole burden of revelation. Gradually, he was creating in his notes the *Spiritual Exercises.*

When, after a year, he left Manresa to make his pilgrimage to Jerusalem, he carried with him the beginnings of his book. He would work on it from 1522 until 1540, but its outline was already clear. So was his fundamental insight into who God really is: His ship to Genoa nearly foundered, and he felt, not fear of God's vengeance and not remorse before the Father, but regret that he had not used his gifts more in God's project.

Having made his way to Jerusalem absolutely destitute, he labored to absorb every physical detail of stone and sky. He had determined to stay there, praying in the holy places and helping souls, available mostly as Turks. The Franciscans, guardians of the Holy Land and used to pilgrim zeal, knew that he would risk slavery or death should he go proselytizing. Iñigo told the ones in charge that he would stay anyhow and risk consequences. The Franciscans felt obliged to let him know about their authority to excommunicate him if he refused to leave. Iñigo did not argue but promptly took ship from Jaffa and after bitter cold and misadventures at sea, arrived in Venice. From there, weaving calmly through battle lines, he returned to Spain, settling in Barcelona.

## Paris and the Study of Theology

Now came a time of waiting and a ten-year period of study. Iñigo felt the need to know more theology. Since that entailed knowing Latin, he sat in grammar school at the age of thirty-three and studied with boys. He continued his lay apostolate of helping souls, sometimes discoursing to small groups and sometimes helping individuals with the Spiritual Exercises. When the friend who was teaching him (and one other; Iñigo appreciated others' opinions) thought he knew enough Latin, he matriculated to the universities at Alcalá and at Salamanca, where he took a hodgepodge of courses and also continued to "help souls." One result was that he gathered a small group of friends.

Another was that, for the first two of a dozen times, he ran afoul of the Inquisition. In later encounters, he would insist on exoneration; now, he overcame by cheerfully remaining in jail and continuing to teach catechism and to give the Spiritual Exercises (Alcalá) and by refusing to escape when all the other prisoners did (Salamanca). The inquisitors examined the book of the *Spiritual Exercises* for the first time and found no harm in it, but were bothered that Iñigo, who freely admitted knowing no theology, taught people to distinguish between deadly and venial sins.

Iñigo received their sentence characteristically: He would not teach people about sin, he said, as long as he remained in their jurisdiction, but their mandate was groundless.

Under this restraint, his earlier decision to study clarified and he chose to go to the center of learning, Paris. Through dead winter in early 1528, once again threading through battle lines, he walked to Paris (he left friends in Barcelona anguished by the rumor that the French were roasting Spaniards on spits). He enrolled at a conservative college, Montaigu, using a name he chose as the Latin equivalent of his own (it is not). More than half way through his life, at thirty-seven, he became Ignatius of Loyola.

At first he somehow found a way to hold spiritual conversations, no doubt often in rough Latin. But he came to recognize that serious study takes time and absorption and renewed his determination to learn. He also came to see that hodgepodge courses lead into confusion; he needed more system. So he moved to a college known for good system, Sainte Barbe, and there completed his study of humanities. He and his Companions, in a matter of fifty years, were to take the seedling of system from Sainte Barbe and cover Europe and the new world with a forest of schools. Ignatius of Loyola would turn out to be one of the world's great educators, his name inscribed in lists along with Maria Montessori and John Dewey.

At Sainte Barbe, he shared rooms with a professor and two others, students who became his first permanent Companions, Pierre Favre of Savoy and Francis Xavier of Navarre. They helped him, half a generation older, to learn philosophy and theology; he helped them learn what they yearned for most. They formed a colleagueship and began attracting others. In 1534, Ignatius directed them through the Spiritual Exercises. Each of them (six by now) lived for a month in a secluded room, except Simón Rodrigues, who spent an hour and a half on the Exercises daily in the midst of his everyday academic life. Each of them elected to do what they had all been talking about for a long time: to live an evangelical life in poverty. Ignatius described the Companions in a letter to a friend simply as "friends in the Lord."

### Friends in the Lord

On August 15, 1534, the Companions gathered on Montmartre and vowed to labor for others while living in poverty. They vowed, further, to go together to Jerusalem and, should that prove impossible, to ask the pope (who would know better?) to send them wherever he thought they could do the most good. Pierre Favre, the only priest among them, celebrated the Mass. Their academic life in this holy fellowship was coming to its end. Ignatius planned to return to Spain (physicians thought his native air would help chronic internal ailments) and then to go wait for the Companions at Venice, the gateway to the Holy Land.

He was getting ready to leave Paris when word came that the *Spiritual Exercises* had once again been denounced to the Inquisition. Ignatius brought his manuscript book to the Inquisitor, a brilliant Dominican to whom Ignatius had presented several reformed people to recant heretical opinions. Having read the manuscript book, the Inquisitor told Ignatius he saw no need for a formal process. Ignatius would not rest but asked him to wait, fetched a scribe, and repeated the whole conversation for the scribe to write out and the Inquisitor to seal.

Then he traveled back to Spain, riding a chestnut horse given him by his friends. He visited his own and some of the Companions' families, made amends in his home for his past sins, preached and mediated disputes, and tried to persuade his priest-brother to live chastely.

Then he left Spain for Venice to wait for the others so that they could make their pilgrimage to the Holy Land. Shaking off the absorption of study, he begged, worked for the poor and the sick, and gave Spiritual Exercises. He also began his deep contemplation again and had spiritual consolations and visions, which had ceased during the years of concentrated study. He was entering on the last part of his life, which he would spend entirely in Italy and, once he reached it, in Rome.

As the Companions completed their degrees or their teaching in Paris, they set out to join him in Venice, traveling through the dangers of the Alpine winter and the battle lines of yet another war. The reunion after nearly two years was very warm. They quickly set to work in the so-called hospitals and poor houses (more like Mother Teresa's hostels for the hopeless dying than our clinics) and started directing others in the Spiritual Exercises and preaching in the churches and even in piazzas. They also befriended the papal legate to Venice and a local bishop. It was the latter who ordained Ignatius and the six others who were not yet priests, in June of 1537. The bishop, Vicenzo Nigusanti, said that no ordination had ever moved him as deeply.

## The Founding of the Company of Jesus

They waited, as they had planned, for a year and then a little more for a ship to sail to the Holy Land. But Christians and Turks were in open war again, and for the first time in thirty years, none sailed. So they fulfilled the last part of their common vow and started for Rome, traveling in trios through the clear Italian fall of 1537.

On the road from Siena down to Rome, at a small shrine always referred to as La Storta, Ignatius and two others stopped to celebrate the Eucharist. As he received Communion (Ignatius would not celebrate Mass until the coming Christmas night), he was given an extraordinary vision that confirmed the decision they had made before leaving Venice to tell anyone who asked that they were the Company of Jesus, like a company of fur traders or of gold seekers or of the king's honor guard. In his vision, Ignatius saw God the Father place him with the Son, accepting them into His service. Ignatius heard the Father promise, "I will be favorable to you all in Rome," which Ignatius thought perhaps meant that they might be crucified there, literally or figuratively. In retrospect, the promise seems to have had less to do with Rome as the place of an event than with Rome as the center of a web of cities newly open to Europeans, like Goa, Kyoto, and Mexico; and of cities just being founded, like Québec, Buenos Aires, and Bogotá. In these other cities, within extraordinarily few years, Companions shaped by the Spiritual Exercises would be working.

The pope, the reformer Paul III, received the Companions and put them to work. Ignatius immediately began inviting legates, high churchmen, and leading lay Romans into the Spiritual Exercises. His Companions also got very active using them, and that gave Ignatius occasion to finish the set of pre-notes he had put together, which he called the "Annotations," and some of the "Norms" in his book.

Two Companions began teaching theology at the request of the pope and all of them went tirelessly to various churches on weekends to hear confessions and to preach. They also began organizing the wealthy for the support of the poor, who were still desperate after the sack of Rome a generation earlier. Particularly during the first winter, 1537–38, severe itself and coming after poor harvests, the Companions helped house, clothe, and feed hundreds of people (a significant percentage of the city's population). Before long, they had launched an orphanage, a home for prostitutes trying to start over and another for girls in danger of turning to prostitution, a refuge for persecuted Jews, and a school to teach everything from the alphabet through the humanities. The school, to the astonishment of the Romans, was free. These efforts for the marginated and poor emerged from the experience of the Spiritual Exercises.

Ignatius began to understand after they had been in Rome just some months that the pope would send the Companions separately out of Rome to perform tasks he judged important. Faced with this prospect, the Companions (now ten) began considering how they would handle separation, which as "friends in the Lord" they appear not to have envisioned. Every day through the Lent of 1539, they prayed and reflected individually and then worked through a sophisticated format for group decision making. They decided to join in a vow to obey the Supreme Pontiff in the place of Christ and to elect one of their own number (for life) whom all would obey as superior general under the pope. They drew up a brief statement of their plan of life, and in the late summer the pope gave it verbal approval. The Vatican took a year to process the decision, since it meant forming another religious order and many opposed that, believing that the reform of existing orders should come first.

Once Pope Paul III gave official approval, in the bull *Regimini militantis ecclesiae* of July 31, 1540, the Companions elected Ignatius superior general. He turned down the first election, so they elected him again, writing the same kind of ballot with a solemn declaration that their candidate was the best before God and men. He turned down the second election, too, and one of the Companions suggested that somebody was resisting the Holy Spirit. Ignatius then went to his Franciscan confessor. He spent the last three days of Holy Week making a confession like the one he began with at Montserrat, and on Easter Sunday he heard the advice to accept.

### The General of the Jesuits

With this, he began fifteen years of administrative life in Rome, years during which his spirituality and mystical prayer came to full maturity. He was commissioned by the Companions to compose the *Constitutions,* the descriptive laws by which the Company of Jesus would grow and govern itself. He worked very slowly for six or seven years and then, with the cooperation of a brilliant associate, Juan de Polanco, produced a document that remains as alive today as the U.S. Constitution. In 1551, he brought some of the original Companions together to study what he had achieved, and when they approved, he sent lieutenants all over Europe to explain the document and to collect reactions and reflections. He refused to consider the *Constitutions* completed until, after his death, the first congregation of senior Companions approved it. They were to do so only in 1558, two years after he had died, delayed by yet more war between Spain and the papacy.

During his term as general, Ignatius accepted nearly a thousand men into the Company. As had all the first Companions, he had planned that most recruits would come from among university people, perhaps ordained or already what the first Companions had been, masters of Paris. But in a matter of four or five years, hundreds of young men caught the Company's fire, and Ignatius recognized the need of founding residences at the universities where they could be trained.

Before long, he was founding schools, not residences. In 1548 — the year the *Spiritual Exercises* were approved by the pope and first printed and the same year that Francis Xavier inaugurated a mission in Japan — after hearing the opinions of just about every Jesuit in or near Rome, Ignatius established the first Jesuit college in Messina, now the University of Messina.

From that year to his death, Ignatius approved about two colleges each year, in Europe and beyond it. In the world new to Europeans, Ignatius was cooperating in the church's instinctive move to education in mission lands. Franciscans had had a school for boys on Hispaniola while Ignatius was learning to write and had established a college in Mexico while he was learning humanities in Paris. Dominicans and Augustinians did the same elsewhere. When Ignatius died, Jesuits were teaching in Goa, Cochin, São Paulo, and other cities.

In Europe, the Company innovated. They appeared with free education (unheard of until then) precisely at the epoch when the towns and cities needed great numbers of literate people to serve the emerging forms of commerce and government. The Company managed to give free education by begging or persuading town corporations, wealthy merchants, or noble rulers to endow the schools (building, books, bed, and board).

Ignatius promoted the *modus Parisiensis,* the orderly system he and others had learned from the Portuguese masters of Sainte Barbe, and elaborated it. He kept Jesuit schools communicating among themselves about what worked and did not work. He set the Company on the road to a system of education, codified at the end of the century as the *Ratio Studiorum,* The Plan of Studies. When one headmaster passed on, the next did not and could not reinvent the school's system, any more than the director of Spiritual Exercises had to with each exercitant. Jesuits became, in even their enemies' opinion, the schoolmasters of Europe.

But Ignatius and the pope set them to other things as large. They sent three of the Companions as theological experts to the Council of Trent, in which they played distinguished roles. Ignatius missioned Peter Canisius to Germany, where he became a major force in church life; sent Nicholas Bobadilla to Poland; and gladly facilitated Paul III's sending Alfonso Salmerón and Pasquase Broët to dampen schism in Ireland. Ignatius wrote into the *Constitutions* that "it is according to our vocation to travel from place to place," looking to do the greater good. He emphatically put that into practice; the only one of the earliest Companions not to travel constantly was Ignatius himself, which must have taxed him since even late in life he thought of himself as "the pilgrim."

When he died in 1556, Ignatius had missioned Jesuits to Africa, India, and Japan and had initiated the missions to the Americas. He had given a structure of government to the Company that reflects the freedom within orderliness characteristic of his Spiritual Exercises and that still functions well in the late twentieth century. He had written seven thousand letters and dozens of directives, leaving behind a larger corpus than any other great founder. Chivvied by his Companions to leave an account of his life, he could barely bring himself to do it, and then told only the beginnings of a bare narrative to one of them with a deep memory and fast quill. Although he did not physically write it, this brief booklet is called the *Autobiography*.

Once he had finished collating his notes on the Spiritual Exercises in 1540, Ignatius wrote almost nothing else on the topic. We have record of only two other people he guided through the experience. He surely never wrote a document his Companions kept asking for: a directory or handbook on how to direct the Spiritual Exercises. He had written all he intended to write on that topic.

❖   **Comment 2**   ❖

# The Book of *Spiritual Exercises*

In 1540, two decades after Leonardo da Vinci's death, a disciple collected the sheaf of notes and sketches that the artist had intended as *A Treatise on Painting*. That same year, Ignatius of Loyola put the final touches on the sheaf of notes that became *Spiritual Exercises*. Four centuries passed before Leonardo's notes were published, and they never have been used to teach others how to paint.

Ignatius's book has a different history. By the time he put final order in his sheaf of notes in Rome, Ignatius had been using them for nearly twenty years. And for several years before 1540, his

Companions had been using them as well. They had been following manuscript notes that Ignatius had given them as he guided
them through the Exercises, which he had either written out for
them or dictated to them. By 1540, scattered away from Rome, they
felt they needed a more certified text.

At the same time, the Companions were being criticized and
yet again denounced to the Inquisition. Ignatius decided that it
would be useful to have official church sanction of the book. This
meant that the text had to be in Latin, the church's and Europe's
official language, and a Latin rather more sure than the simple
text, probably his own, that Ignatius had been using since Paris,
where everyone spoke it. So Ignatius secured one and then another translation by scholarly Companions (one was a famous
humanist, André des Freux) and brought them both to the Vatican. Paul III gave an unusually solemn approval in 1548 with a
papal brief. That same year, the text was printed, but not published; it was meant for use only by Jesuits and Ignatius kept the
five hundred copies under his own control.

It has not been controlled since. Exactly four centuries after this
first printing, leading authorities estimated that the *Spiritual Exercises* had been printed the equivalent of once a month during all
that time. If anything, the frequency has increased, particularly in
this century as translations have appeared in many languages.

### The Practice of the Exercises

Ignatius's *Spiritual Exercises* (the book) has been in constant use
now for 450 years, as tens of thousands have gone through the
month of the Exercises (the experience). We might say this con-
cretely: Ignatius took Pierre Favre through the Spiritual Exercises.
Favre directed Jerónimo Domènech, who then directed Diego
Mirón. Mirón became expert at guiding others and directed an
Italian youth who joined the Company. In his time, that youth directed another youth who joined the Company, and so on. The
ways of guiding and directing changed, but the very real linkage
has continued for more than four and a half centuries, down to the
writer of this commentary, who made a permanent life commitment through the Exercises four decades ago and has since guided
others who have done and are doing the same.

Like da Vinci's book, *Spiritual Exercises* is a handbook: Ignatius wrote only about the person making and the person directing the Exercises, sketching out what they might do and how they might proceed. Unlike da Vinci, he included no embracing theory. He did not, consequently, elaborate a theology of spiritual development, as his young contemporary John of the Cross would later. In this respect, his handbook differs entirely from John Calvin's *Institutes*, published in 1536. That guide to truly Christian believing and living is a full exploration of all Christian doctrine — in four volumes. Ignatius adduced theology only when he wanted to clarify or to emphasize some practical directive.

The reason for his reticence in exploring theology is, in part, very plain: Ignatius had finished the substance of the book while still a layman and uninstructed in theology. His notable devotions to the Mass, the sacraments, and the saints were all solidly centrist doctrines commonly held and taught in Spain. The few more advanced theological positions that he held, such as that the Holy Spirit deals directly with each person, were well within the church's tradition. Before Ignatius even knew about the growing controversies on grace and on justification, he had learned the basic doctrine concerning them from soundly trained confessors and spiritual directors among Dominicans, Benedictines, and Carthusians.

## The Spiritual Tradition of the West

Ignatius's spiritual theology developed under the influence of several strong traditions in the West. His early Companions felt that his grasp of theology came more from the Holy Spirit than from books, but the fact is that his conversion at thirty-one took shape as he read and reread two books. The first was a deeply devout *Life of Christ* written by Ludolph of Saxony, a Carthusian who had done excellent theological studies as a Dominican. He brought to Iñigo the influence of the Rhineland mystics John Tauler and Henry Suso and prepared him to find life-long devotion in Thomas à Kempis's *Imitation of Christ*. The piety Ludolph represented, the *devotio moderna*, left behind earlier centuries' taste for speculative theology and showed little interest in dogmatic theology. It tended to be less intellectual and more humbly affective. Above all, it turned in deep devotion to Jesus Christ. Ludolph placed Christ at the center of life, all things ordered around Him and in Him.

The second book the recuperating Iñigo absorbed was the lives of some saints written by an Italian Dominican, Jacobus de Voragine. The book had been translated into Spanish and adapted by a member of an austere eremitical order, and a long preface was provided for it by a Cistercian, Gauberto Vagad. It is marked by devotion to Jesus Christ and a thirst to imitate Him. In reading it, Iñigo felt a deep attraction to the *life* of the saints. As he followed their stories, he found himself attracted to doing great and outstanding deeds in service of God our Creator and Lord.

At Manresa, the author of *Spiritual Exercises* came under the influence of a centuries-old way of living an interior life aided by what were explicitly called "spiritual exercises." Authors had at first used the phrase to refer simply to reading and pondering Scripture or meditating in general. But by Ignatius's time, they had come to apply it to an organized scheme of growth in the interior life. The penitent Iñigo used such a book written by Abbot García Jiménez de Cisneros and printed at Montserrat in 1500, *Exercises for the Spiritual Life*. This manual for the spiritual life aims at growing through the purgative, illuminative, and the unitive ways. Ignatius adopted the terms, but the purpose of his Spiritual Exercises is more focused, and they are intended for use during a limited time. The structure of *Spiritual Exercises*, though he borrowed the term "Weeks" to indicate its four sections, is entirely his own.

## A Spirituality for the Day

The spirituality tersely expressed in this book was extraordinarily helpful to the sixteenth-century church. Christians were emerging from medieval spirituality into the Renaissance and from a Europe besieged by the infidel into a world that seemed to have no boundaries. Christians leading ordinary lives in this struggling world, lay and clerical, found the old forms of religion and piety no great match for their needs. They felt keen concern for their personal redemption in a world that appeared dyed deeply with sin. The more spiritual felt a terrible responsibility to save themselves from Hell, to put order into the church, and to bring Christ to the perishing infidel. They were discovering a great devotion to the human Jesus, particularly to the suffering Savior.

Into this world, Ignatius and his Companions introduced a spirituality that begins in a resounding affirmation: All comes from God, all moves under God's governance and care, all returns to God, in and through Christ Jesus. Our first task is reverent gratitude. But we are to express that gratitude in action; we are given both responsibility to act and the power to act. As the Lord Jesus did, so we must act always in service of others. It is in enactment that we find God, but unless we are contemplative we will miss God acting in everything around us and in our selves. We can always know what we are to do for love of God; we can always know best by imitating Jesus Christ.

Today we find ourselves in a situation analogous to that of Ignatius and his contemporaries. We are anxious about our salvation, though our anxiety finds expression in terms of emergence and self-realization. We find our life world plagued with wars and wretchedness, and we sense a pervasive wrongness in social and economic structures that can rightly be called sin. We live in an age when limits have been broken and boundaries have been leveled in every dimension, by depth psychology, communication technologies, revolutionary movements, and space travel. We feel a keen need for order and for a way to find some meaning in human life beyond the mere consumption of goods. And in the study of Scripture, we have rediscovered Jesus of Nazareth.

Probably in greater numbers than at any time during the past four centuries, men and women find Ignatian spirituality relevant to their interior lives and pertinent to their lives as Christians and as church members. Certainly, they are making the Spiritual Exercises in greater numbers than anywhere recorded, all around the globe.

✤ **Comment 3** ✤

# The Experience
# of Spiritual Exercises

The first mark on the Autograph copy of the *Spiritual Exercises* is this symbol: IHS. The letters, used as the monogram of the Company of Jesus, abbreviate the Greek form of Jesus' name, IESOUS. It is at the top of these pages to indicate the world in which the Spiritual Exercises proceed. They do not begin in philosophy and end in theology, or begin in stoicism and end in mysticism. The Spiritual Exercises begin and end in life in Christ.

This life in Christ Ignatius understood as life in the visible church. Everything exists in Christ, and everything existing in Christ pertains to the life of the church in some way. Ignatius was not "churchly"; he and the Companions resolutely refused often-proffered bishoprics, distrusted fixed incomes (benefices), stripped liturgy to bare reverence and meaning, loved the company of unbelievers and lapsed Catholics, and spent much unclerical time with plague victims, prostitutes, and the poor. But Ignatius saw all grace coming from God into humankind through the church, broken and corrupted, as a whole symphony must come from an orchestra, however inattentive, unskilled, and ill-equipped.

The Spiritual Exercises, therefore, function within the structure of the church, and they are a structured religious experience. Though we eagerly look for freedom through the structured experiences of psychiatric counsel, of twelve-step programs, and of human empowerment workshops, we tend to fear structured religious experiences as repressive and constricting. But as you pray through the Exercises, you find that they come from and elicit a profound human freedom and a profound experience of God.

This is what Ignatius hoped to help people to do, and he gave help in several ways. Those whom he considered able and ready for it, he would invite to spend a month alone, in seclusion, under his direction, as he did Francis Xavier in a little room away from the University of Paris. Later on, he walked eighty miles through the hills south of Rome to the monastery at Monte Cassino, where he and a Scripture professor from Salamanca, Pedro Ortiz, were housed by the Benedictines while the professor went through the Exercises (they spent forty days).

## The Long, or Thirty-Day, Retreat

Ignatius explains something about his practice in Annotation 20 [20]. (The paragraphs of Ignatius's text are referred to by numbers in brackets.) We still follow his practice, though ordinarily in a retreat house in suburb or country. You agree to withdraw from all other activities, keep deep silence, and spend about thirty full days in prayer, reading, and reflection. You pray in the several ways noted in Comment 20; you probably diet and deny other appetites; and you ignore news media, telephone, and mail. You come to understand that the more you pull away from every current reality in your life and the further you go into silence, the more fully and deeply you encounter your authentic self and God in Christ. You will hear this experience called in current argot "the long retreat" or "the thirty-day retreat."

Your thirty-day retreat will be divided into what are called the Four Weeks, though they do not last seven days each [4]. After preparing for a few days, you move through the Weeks. You consider God's mercy and humankind's sin in the First Week, Jesus' Incarnation and public life in the Second, His Passion and death in the Third, and His Resurrection and continued life in the world in the Fourth. You go to Mass daily and perhaps join other liturgical prayer.

Every day you pray four or five full hours at times you set [12]. Most days, you discover presently, you rise in the middle of the night to keep one of those hours. At noon and at night, you will examine how you are doing and renew your decision to be wholehearted [1, 12]. You also find yourself urged to say other prayers, perhaps psalms or hours of the Divine Office, and at some point do some reading, for example, in lives of the saints. You may do other exercises that your director suggests as the two of you sense what you need [17].

You see your director regularly, which to Ignatius meant daily or every two days, as it does to current directors. What do you talk about? In broad strokes, what has gone on in your prayer, how desires and decisions are shaping up, and whether you find your faith and trust in God stronger or less strong [13]. Your director will be particularly keen to know whether you feel up or down, in good spirits or dejected. He or she is very likely to talk with you about how "spirits" affect your behavior, attitudes, thinking, and valuing [6, 8, 10]. In detail, you might indicate whether any ideas, emotions, or desires moved you, and what insights you had into your self or your life world. You and your director will explore at various times the materials Ignatius incorporates throughout the book, for instance, in "Norms Followed in Discerning Spirits" [313–27 and 228–36]. As you end your session, which may be ten minutes or fifty, you receive the materials for the next day from your director, who gives you a bare sketch, oral or written, of their substance [2, 11].

Do you tell your director about your sins? Well, keep very clear the distinction among therapy, confession, and spiritual direction. In therapy, you must mention whatever comes to mind by way of free association, and deliberate holding back interferes with the healing process. In confession, you must tell a priest in detail what you have done or left undone contrary to your own conscience. In Ignatian spiritual direction, you choose what to tell your director about your experiences in prayer and silence, what you are doing and what you are desiring. Your director helps you interpret those experiences. Hence, during your thirty-day retreat, you recount what moves you: emotions, affects, thoughts, images, and yearnings that encourage or dishearten you, including those that you recognize as temptations to sin [17]. The more complete and detailed you are, the better your director can help.

### The Exercitant: Those Who Go through the Exercises

Ignatius stressed that the Exercises are to be carefully adapted to the person going through them [18]. He also insisted on selectivity: He was most interested in gifted men and women who were generous and big-hearted enough to dedicate their lives to serve people, in public life or in the church. He also thought it most useful to pursue people in positions of authority, to straighten out their lives and purify their service. He did not judge merely by externals: One of his last exercitants was an illiterate.

Most of the people making the thirty-day retreat today have

an education and gifts that are beyond the ordinary. You do not need theological training, but if you are going to work out for yourself the meaning of revelation in Christ [2], you must have some religious sophistication. You are strong-minded enough to look hard at the brokenness of humanity and at your own woundedness and to feel the burden of that sorrow without disintegrating or regressing. You need not, by the way, be Catholic; the first Jesuits worked with some who were not, particularly in northern Europe, and directors today commonly accompany people from other churches.

You do need a developed religious sensibility, for you will be asked, to give an instance, to notice that you can be drawn to evil under the guise of good [10]. You will be asked to notice consolations and desolations in your prayer, and to learn how to identify the spiritual forces behind these movements in your spirit [6]. You need a kind of hardihood in your introspection, for should you find yourself unreasonably drawn to something, say popularity or monied success, you will be encouraged to beg God the Lord to give you a great desire for anything but that, so that you can be free from the unreasonableness [16].

As will emerge later, you may come to the Exercises in order to elect how to spend your life (married, single, priesthood, a religious institute) or in order to make some serious choices about career or lifestyle (career change, further education, finding your way out of a seriously sinful situation). You may also be someone simply ready to make some decisions in your interior life and eager to grow in your relationship with God, to "make progress," as Ignatius regularly puts it.

Whatever brings you to them, you come best to the Spiritual Exercises with a great spirit, looking boldly for *more*, a larger way to live and serve, something bigger to do than the ordinary [5].

### Annotation 19: Exercises at Home

Among women and men who had these qualifications, Ignatius found some whom he wished to guide through the Exercises and who wanted to make them, but who could not go off for a month [19]. A nobleman, for instance, could not leave his household; a doctor of theology could not leave his teaching. Keeping at their routine, such persons would set aside a significant period of time each day to do the Exercises. They would spend an hour in prayer in the morning and a quarter of an hour at noon and at night examining their behavior and their attitudes. It was common enough in Ignatius's time for serious people to pray daily in their homes, as it is in ours, so such people would just take up the Exercises. Ignatius used this method with people of whom he thought a great deal; Simon Rodrigues, one of the first Jesuit Companions, is a prime instance.

This is an important point at the end of the twentieth century, because many women and men are open to experience the Exercises who cannot go off to the country for a month. They are making "nineteenth-annotation retreats," or "Exercises at home," in current terms. They may continue for some months or as long as a year, handling serious options about state in life, career, or lifestyle. They may go through the experience along with a group of others, but the more serious their intentions, the more likely they are to have an individual director.

Ignatius sometimes started helping through the Exercises a person who turned out to lack the stamina or deep enough desire required to go through the whole experience. When he recognized that, breathing no breath of a judgmental attitude, Ignatius would gently break off before starting the difficult days of election or decision in the Second Week. He explains this in the second half of Annotation 18.

He also found many people whom he wanted to help but who had slight gifts of interior prayer or of systematic spiritual activity. He would hold conversations with them or chat with them over a period of time, following the materials of the first days of the Exercises concerning God creating and forgiving our sin. He did this especially early on in Alcalá and Salamanca, for instance, with individuals and also with groups. His followers continued his practice in Rome, Parma, Coimbra, Cologne, and elsewhere. To suggest the level implied here, Ignatius sometimes referred to this as "teaching catechism," and placed first in his book the exercises he used for it. He describes what he did in the first half of Annotation 18.

## The Preached Retreat

Historically, the outline of revealed truth provided by the Four Weeks of the *Spiritual Exercises* proved an enduring contribution to Western spirituality. From very early on, Ignatius's Companions used it as a framework for every kind of religious communication. The one whom Ignatius considered the best director, Pierre Favre, preached the Exercises to groups more than once. During Ignatius's lifetime, a Jesuit in Italy taught priests Scripture by preaching his way through the materials of the Exercises. Jesuits in the sixteenth century and ever since have produced books of religious instruction and what we would call spiritual reading by simply writing out sermons and reflections based on the sequence of meditations.

In the directed retreat, whether thirty days or at home, the director does not preach; he or she gives just a sketch of the materials for prayer [2]. But by the time Pilgrim and Puritan had begun preaching in New England, Jesuits were preaching retreats as well as directing them. They would give a series of sermons, perhaps five a day, based on each of the meditations and contemplations in its sequence.

Jesuits directed individuals and preached to groups for two centuries. Then, just as the United States was forming itself, in 1773, the Company of Jesus was put out of existence by papal decree (except in Russia) and was not restored until Napoleon had shattered the politics of Europe, in 1814. With that restoration, the preached retreat seems to have become more common than the directed retreat.

During the nineteenth century and until the Second Vatican Council, Jesuits tended to preach even the thirty-day retreat, even to their own novices and priests. Instead of meeting each exercitant once a day and letting him or her pray five hours, they preached to a group five times a day, perhaps for only twenty minutes but often for much longer, after which the exercitants would finish the hour praying over what they had heard.

During the nineteenth century, too, many congregations of sisters, brothers, and priests began going through the Spiritual Exercises during their training. As the century wore on, they also took on the Jesuit custom of making a compressed form of the Exercises for about a week each calendar year, almost always preached. A great German Jesuit preacher was rattling religious' complacency in these retreats while Bismarck rattled their politics. Right through the Second World War, Jesuits all around the world were preaching retreats to convents and groups of priests for five, eight, and thirty days.

During the early twentieth century, Jesuits began preaching weekend retreats for laymen and then women, and the women Religious of the Cenacle took for their service in the church conducting Ignatian retreat houses for women. Their practice was not new; Jesuits in France had been doing this for audiences while Shakespeare was declaiming his plays in London. In this century, they began opening retreat houses, hotel-like residences where people could spend the weekend in silence, listening four or five times a day to a director expound the meditations in sequence.

These preached retreats, which regularly effect genuine change in people's lives, are the Spiritual Exercises most people today are familiar with. Many Catholic men and women, particularly those who finished college before the end of the Eisenhower years, remember going off to a retreat house to listen to a preacher for three days in silence. For a very long time, Jesuits tended to follow this one line of their tradition and left directed retreats aside.

## The Annotations

This entailed an incomplete reading of the twenty important prenotes that Ignatius had written, the "Annotations." These instructions nowhere explicitly state that the director meets one-on-one with the exercitant, but the implication is inescapable even if the history were not clear. These Annotations, therefore, are principally about directed retreats, though they contain sound spiritual doctrine applicable elsewhere.

Ignatius had learned how to help people as he preached to and directed them over a period of twenty years. He knew that some of these lessons — such as when to use the Sacrament of Reconciliation — could be noted best at the juncture in the Exercises when they applied. But some things, either about the director or about the one going through the Exercises, he considered of primary importance. These he gathered into the Annotations without putting any special order into them.

The Annotations, as you will see, imply that a director needs a rather strong grasp of the way the human spirit moves in and out of darkness and light, joy in the Lord and sorrow, clarity and confusion. The entire enterprise of inviting someone to pray through the Spiritual Exercises might also seem to suggest a director with a better than ordinary background in philosophy, psychology, Scripture, and theology. But just at this point we should remember that Ignatius of Loyola, when he had the basic experiences embodied in these Exercises and wrote down the main burden of them, was still an only slightly educated layman.

He had a world of piety and spirituality by heart and said constantly a prayer focused almost fiercely on Jesus Christ, that he recommends often during the Spiritual Exercises:

> Soul of Christ, make me holy
> Body of Christ, redeem me
> Blood of Christ, inebriate me
> Water from Christ's side, cleanse me
> Passion of Christ, make me strong
> O Good Jesus, hear me
> Hide me in your wounds
> Never let me depart from you
> Defend me from the evil enemy
> Call me at the hour of my death
> Bid me come to you
> That with your saints I may praise you
> Forever and ever. Amen.

✤ **Ignatian Text** ✤

# I H S [1]
# Annotations

*These pre-notes are meant to give some understanding of the Spiritual Exercises that follow. They should prove helpful to the one who gives the Exercises and also to the one who goes through them.*

The First Annotation. This Annotation defines the term "Spiritual Exercises." Here it includes every kind of self-examination, of meditation, of contemplation, of vocal and mental prayer, and of other spiritual activities, as explained further along.

As strolling, walking along a road, and running are physical exercises, so all of these — getting ready for and committing one's self to break all disordered attachments, and then (once the attachments are broken) seeking and finding what God wishes in one's life — are called "Spiritual Exercises."

The Second. The person who gives another the method and [2] order for making a meditation or a contemplation should accurately tell the salvation story that belongs to that meditation or contemplation. He should do no more than remark briefly and concisely on the points given. The rationale is this: When the one contemplating takes his start from the basic salvation story and works through it reflectively for himself, he may well discover something that helps him understand that saving event more fully or appreciate it better. Now, whether he achieves insight by his own natural reasoning or is given insight by divine action, he gets more spiritual satisfaction and fulfillment this way than he would have gotten had the one giving the exercise explicated the meaning of the salvation story and given it a lengthy development. For it is not knowing a lot, but grasping things intimately and savoring them that fills and satisfies the soul.

The Third. Since in all of the Spiritual Exercises included here [3] we set our minds in motion to comprehend and our wills in action to freely feel and value, we need to notice this: Whenever we exercise our free affectivity, as in speaking out loud or in our hearts with God our Lord or with the saints, we have to mark our actions with greater reverence than when we set our minds to think things through.

[4]    The Fourth. Four Weeks are assigned for the Exercises that follow, corresponding to the four parts into which the Exercises are divided: the First, the consideration and contemplation of sin; the Second, the life of Christ our Lord through Palm Sunday; the Third, the Passion of Christ our Lord; the Fourth, the Resurrection and the Ascension (to which "Three Methods of Praying" is added). Calling them "Weeks," however, does not mean that they have to last exactly seven full days. For experiences differ: In the First Week, for instance, some find more slowly than others what they want (viz., contrition, sorrow, and tears for their sins); some try harder than others; some are more stirred up and tested by various spirits. As a consequence, in some cases the First Week should be shortened and in others it should be lengthened. The same holds for each of the other three Weeks and the search for appropriate personal experience of their subject matters. For all that, the Exercises ought to last just about thirty days.

[5]    The Fifth. The person who goes through the Exercises will gain a great deal by going into them with a wide open spirit, generous toward his Creator and Lord, offering to God all his desiring and his freedom to choose, so that the Divine Majesty can freely call upon him and make use of all he has in realizing His most holy wishes.

[6]    The Sixth. When the one who gives the Exercises senses that an exercitant is experiencing no spiritual movements like consolations or desolations and is not being stirred by one spirit or another, then he ought to ply him with questions about his Exercises: whether he makes the Exercises at the scheduled times and how he does them. He should ask, going point by point, whether the exercitant is following the Additions punctiliously.

Consolation and desolation are explained in [316–24], and the Additions, in [73–89].

[7]    The Seventh. Should the one who gives the Exercises observe that the one who makes them feels desolate and tempted, he would not then deal harshly and severely with him, but gently and kindly, encouraging him and giving him the heart to keep on.

He should shed light on the wily maneuvers of humanity's enemy and get him to open himself to and get ready for consolation, which will come.

The Eighth. As the one who gives the Exercises senses in the [8] one going through them a need to understand his experiences of desolations and the wily maneuvers of the enemy, and of consolations as well, he will do well to talk over with him the "Norms Followed in Discerning Spirits" for the First Week and for the Second Week [313–27] and [328–36].

The Ninth. Here is something to notice about a person going [9] along in the Exercises of the First Week. Suppose this person, not very experienced in spiritual matters, suffers gross, blunt temptations as he sees looming before him the obstacles to continuing to grow in the service of God, things like hard struggles, being shamed, threats to his worldly status, and so on. With a person in this case, the one who gives the Exercises would not talk over the Norms about the diverse spirits for the Second Week. The fact is, these Norms are too subtle and advanced for him to grasp; they will do him a lot of harm, whereas the Norms for the First Week will give him a lot of help.

The Tenth. When the one who gives the Exercises senses that [10] the one going through them is being assailed and tempted by what appears as a good, then he appropriately talks with him about the Norms for the Second Week that have been mentioned. For when a person goes along practicing the illuminative way (which corresponds to the Exercises of the Second Week), human nature's enemy ordinarily tempts him under the guise of good, which the enemy does not often do during the purgative way (which corresponds to the Exercises of the First Week).

The Eleventh. It is an advantage to a person going through the [11] Exercises of the First Week, to know nothing of what he faces in the Second Week. He needs to work at getting the good that he seeks in the First Week as though he expected to find nothing good in the Second.

The Twelfth. The one who gives the Exercises should impress [12] this on the one who is going through them: Since he has to spend an hour in each one of the five meditations or contemplations assigned every day, he should gauge himself so that at the end of every Exercise he feels quite confident that he has spent a full hour on it, tending to go longer than an hour rather than to stop short of it. The reason is that the enemy all too often contrives to get the hour of contemplation, meditation, or prayer shortened.

[13]    The Thirteenth. Along the same line, we need to note this: It is easy and light work to contemplate for the full hour during a time of consolation; during a time of desolation, it is quite difficult to stay the full hour. In light of this, a person going through the Exercises, in order to struggle against his desolations and overcome his temptations, ought to stay a little longer than the hour. In this way, he gets used not only to fighting back against the enemy, but to defeating him.

[14]    The Fourteenth. If the one who gives the Exercises notices that an exercitant is going through them with consolation and a lot of fervor, then he needs to warn that person against making any rash, hasty promise or vow. The more unstable he has come to see the person's character, the more he ought to advise and warn him.

Granted that it is quite correct to urge one or another person to enter religious life, where the vows of obedience, poverty, and chastity are made; and granted that a good work done because of a vow is more meritorious than a good work done without a vow. Nevertheless, the one giving the Exercises must consider closely the actual circumstances and character of the person taking a vow, and how many helps and hindrances he might find in fulfilling the promise he wants to make.

[15]    The Fifteenth. The one who gives the Exercises should move an exercitant neither to embrace poverty or take some vow, nor to do the opposites, and no more into one way of or state in life than into another. Outside of the time of the Spiritual Exercises, admittedly, we can lawfully and meritoriously encourage everyone who seems fit to choose continence, virginity, a life in religion, and any way of life leading to evangelical perfection. During the time of the Exercises, on the contrary, it is more appropriate and altogether better in the search for God's will that the Creator and Lord directly communicate Himself to a deeply committed person, enfolding him in God's love and praise and getting him ready to go ahead onto the way in which he will be more able to serve God. This surely means that the one who gives the Exercises holds himself in equilibrium like a truly balanced scale, leaning neither to one side nor to the other, allowing the Creator to deal directly with the one being created and the one being created directly with the Creator.

The Sixteenth. Here is something further to ensure that the [16] Creator and Lord be the one at work in this creation of His. It can sometimes happen that a person feels strong, disordered inclination and attachment to something. When that happens, it will be very profitable for him to stir all his powers and set himself to grow to the opposite attachment and inclination. Suppose, for instance, that a person feels attached to pursuing and holding a certain office or benefice; and he wants this for his own advantage and in his own temporal interest, not for the honor and glory of God our Lord or in the interest of others' spiritual well-being. This person has to reverse the way he is attached. In insistent prayers and other spiritual exercises, he must insist and plead with God our Lord that he wants the contrary, which is to say that he will seek neither this office or benefice nor any other thing whatsoever, unless God in His Majesty, putting order into his desiring, transmute his original attachment. Then, the source of his desiring, the purpose why he goes after one or other thing, will be purely the service, honor, and glory of His Divine Majesty.

The Seventeenth. Though the one who gives the Exercises [17] entertains no desire to seek out and know the private thoughts and the personal sins of the one making the Exercises, nonetheless, it is very useful that he be told faithfully about the various incitements and thoughts caused by the actions of the various spirits. With this information, he can give appropriate exercises that match greater or lesser progress and respond to the needs of this particular person being awakened this way.

The Eighteenth. The Spiritual Exercises have to be adapted to [18] the conditions of the persons who want to make them, conditions like age, education, and talent. Plainly, materials would not be given to an uneducated person or to one with a fragile make-up that he cannot handle without being worn out and from which he would not derive much profit. By the same token, each person should be given any exercises that he willingly makes himself ready for and open to, so that he can find more help and make better progress.

Consequently, should a person wish no further help than some instruction and the achievement of some peace of soul, he would be given the Particular Examination of Conscience [24–31], and then the General Examination of Conscience [32–43]. To this might be added the method of praying for a half-hour each morning on the Commandments and on the Seven Deadly Sins [238–45], and the rest [246–60]. Also, weekly confession should be suggested to him and, if he can, Communion every two weeks or even every week, if he is disposed to that.

This method is more suitable to those who have little ability or are illiterate. It involves explaining to them each of the Commandments, the Seven Deadly Sins, and the Commandments of the church; the use of the five senses; and the works of mercy.

A similar situation rises when the one who gives the Exercises learns that the one going through them has a weak character or little natural ability and cannot be expected to produce much. He could more appropriately give such a person some of the above-mentioned easier exercises, working up to the confession of his sins. Then, he should give him some ways of examining his conscience and a program for more frequent confession than he has been used to, so that he can maintain what he has gained.

The one who gives these exercises ought not go on to the material about election, or to any other of the Exercises beyond the First Week, particularly when he can elicit greater growth in others and there is not enough time to do everything.

[19]     The Nineteenth. A person caught up in public affairs or in occupations that he cannot interrupt, if he is educated or clearly gifted, can make the Exercises by taking an hour and a half each day. The one who gives the Exercises should talk through what men are being created for. Then for half an hour, he can explain the Particular Examination of Conscience, then the General Examination of Conscience, and then a method of confessing and of receiving Communion.

The one going through Exercises should spend an hour on the first, second, and third sins [45–54], three days in a row. Then at the same hour on another three days, he should ponder the indictment of his own sins [55–61]; and on still another three days, the punishment due to sins [65–71]. For these meditations, he should be given the ten Additions [73–89].

He would follow the same pattern in meditating on the mysteries of the life of Christ our Lord, explained at length further on in the Exercises.

[20]     The Twentieth. A person who is less occupied and who wants to profit as much as possible should be given all of these Spiritual Exercises in the exact order given here. He will profit more, as a

general rule, the more he distances himself from all his friends and relations and from worldly concerns. For instance, he might move out of his present quarters into another house (or another room, anyhow), so that he can live there in as great privacy as possible, and also so that he can go to daily Mass and to Vespers without having to worry that acquaintances will prove obstacles.

By distancing himself this way, a person gets three particular benefits, among a lot of others:

First, when for the sake of serving and praising God our Lord a person distances himself from all his friends and relations and at the same time from a lot of busyness that is not well ordered, he gains no little merit in the eyes of His Divine Majesty.

Second, when a person distances himself this way, his mind is not scattered onto many concerns; he focuses his concern on one thing only, serving his Creator and growing in his own spirit. The upshot is that he enjoys a freer use of his natural powers as he seriously searches for what he so much desires.

Third, the more a person finds himself alone and apart, the more ready he finds himself to approach and be united with his Creator and Lord. And the more he unites himself to God, the more he disposes himself to receive graces and gifts from His divine and supreme Goodness.

❖ **Comment 4** ❖

# Spiritual Doctrine
# in the *Spiritual Exercises*

You begin the thirty-day Exercises by resting for three or four days, or for as many weeks if you are doing the Exercises at home, in the spiritual doctrine that guides your life. You believe in God the almighty Creator; so what? You expect life after death; what difference has that made in your everyday life? If you have known your director for a while, you may already have spent time on the spiritual import of the truths of Revelation, in prayer, and in discourse. Whether you have or not, you now spend some quiet days placing yourself in the middle of Revelation. These are your preparation days.

Several rather central points in the church's beliefs hide in the book's title, a sentence fragment [21], and in the two brief paragraphs following it, one left untitled but generally called "Presupposition" [22], and the other titled "Principle and Foundation" [23]. The beliefs give fundamental shape to the experience of the Spiritual Exercises.

### The Title-like Sentence Fragment

The title of a book in Ignatius's time was commonly long and often ended with its author's name and qualifications. Ignatius wrote a title like that but did not add either his name or his qualification, master of Paris [21]. He was asked by his secretary, Juan de Polanco, as the book was being prepared for the printer whether he should be identified as the author. Ignatius left the choice to his secretary. Consequently, the title page of the first printing had simply *Spiritual Exercises*, the Company's seal with its IHS, and the year, 1548. The secretary, remaining anonymous himself, named Ignatius as author in a brief preface.

The title-like sentence uses two dated expressions: "to gain mastery over one's self" and "disordered affects." Much of what we say about the "self" today, Ignatius and his contemporaries said about the "soul." Ignatius and his contemporaries conceived of the soul as fully present from the moment of birth, a treasure to be guarded until judgment. The individual had an end to attain, eternal life for that soul, and every human action was a means to that end. As Englishmen at the time of Ignatius's conversion were reading in the Bibles placed by Thomas Cromwell in every parish church: "For what is a man profited, if he shall gain the whole world, and lose his own soul? or what shall a man give in exchange for his soul?" (Matt. 16:26).

How did a person save his or her soul? By keeping the Commandments and church law, and obeying the legitimate rulings of authorities. This developed virtues and defended against vices, which were expressions of the fully existing soul preparing itself for eternal happiness or eternal woe. A deeply committed person enjoyed a sense of conforming to objective reality defined by tradition, and when he or she was pulled away from objective virtue, there was question of some disordered desiring and commitment.

That disordered desiring and commitment is what Ignatius means by a "disordered affect." He did not mean an emotion, merely, like the feeling of fear in the stormy dark or of hunger in the morning. Rather, any affect includes the valuing, feeling, and desiring that follows on a commitment. Say you commit yourself seriously to a team research project. You feel great eagerness and work sixty-hour weeks and would be repelled to be left out of anything important in the process. Your eagerness and your repugnance are affects that follow on and flow from your serious commitment.

We are not perfectly consistent, of course. Suppose you also had a prior commitment to a spouse and large family before you took up the team project. Then your eagerness for it, which leads you to spend exorbitant amounts of time away from your family, would plainly not be ordered according to your prior commitment. The eagerness, therefore, would be what Ignatius called a "disordered affect." It confuses your priorities and your desiring and may ultimately lead you to choose against your own conscience. You have grown deeply attached to that team project and you are hurting your spouse and family.

As Ignatius's sentence suggests, you will find help in these Spiritual Exercises to identify the disordered affects that you harbor and to escape their influence as you come to serious election or choices. You find that merely knowing yourself better this way gives a sense of order in your life. Being offered the courage to gain some rational management of your affects — that's part of the self-mastery — gives an even deeper sense of order.

## A Presupposition

The next paragraph in the *Spiritual Exercises* [22] has to do with mutual understanding between the exercitant and the director. Ignatius gave no indication about how he used it or why he put it here. He composed the paragraph in Paris and authorities tend to believe that the sentences may reflect his experiences with the

Inquisition (he was examined, he once wrote to King John of Portugal, eight times).

Whatever his reason for writing it, Ignatius calls dramatic attention by the paragraph to the basic process of the Spiritual Exercises: listening. The exercitant listens to the Spirit of God and to the director. The director listens to the exercitant, to his or her own experience and learning, and in everything to the same Spirit. Plainly, their listening is dialogic.

The dialogue Ignatius urges in the Presupposition describes what psychologists now call "active listening." Elements in this process show up in Annotations 6 and 17, but Annotation 15 says plainly why director and exercitant listen to each other: The Holy Spirit communicates directly not only with the whole bent world and the whole church but with each and every individual. This belief in the Spirit's communication was not the heresy of another lay movement in Spain, the illuminism of *Los Alumbrados*. They surely believed that the Holy Spirit illumined each person, but they were anti-sacraments, anti-intellect, and waited passively for God. Ignatius's beliefs could hardly be more different. His stance, the ground of the "active listening" described here, affirms the Spirit's work through the sacraments and in and through intellect. And you may wait upon God during the Exercises, but you will be laboring to prepare until God comes.

The listening of the director, the foundational activity in directing the Spiritual Exercises, is not merely sincere and random. If structure in listening is important for psychotherapists, it is even more important for spiritual directors. Ignatian spiritual directors have been formed by the experience of Spiritual Exercises and have continually studied the book. They have intentionally adopted an elaborated spirituality, one of the church's several ways of perceiving, evaluating, and discerning spiritual experience: consolation and desolation, humility and great desires, the sources of illumination and decision. Within this consciously and reflectively chosen spirituality, he or she can hear what you say accurately and interact personally and yet keep his or her own interests from contaminating yours. For this reason, a sensible director will have mastered these Spiritual Exercises before trying to help you.

## The Principle and Foundation

In the mystical illumination at the River Cardoner, Ignatius was given deep insight into how all creatures come from God in Christ and return to God in Christ. God is carrying out a great project in which each human person contributes in concrete ways that God has specifically hoped for. The Creator can teach us those ways, what to Ignatius was "God's will," so each can know the end for which God moment by moment creates him or her. This end or aim, far from an abstraction, comes out of and is realized in our concrete gifts and the determining circumstances of our lives, which are also creatures being created moment by moment by the same God. When I know myself thoroughly, I can know what I am for: whether to marry or to live celibate, to accept power or to work quietly, to pursue learning or wealth or simplicity or poverty.

I will never know myself, however, until I agree that God is my Maker and creates me to some end, placing in me an original purpose that I will discover in my concrete self and life world and in the dialogue of desiring, and not create on my own. This is the meaning of being a creature; to attempt anything different is to try to make yourself a god, and absurd.

Recall that Ignatius perceived the self as already whole when a person comes to decide what to do with her or his life, so that he saw that self striving to reach an established final end. We think differently, in terms of evolution and process. We perceive the self incomplete, unfolding, coming to be. Consequently, we tend to think rather of an "original purpose" than of a "final end." The true shape of the rose is already in its bud; the mature shape of any embryo is already in the DNA of its first multiplying cells. Analogously, my authentic self — the self who will, God hopes, live forever — is already in my concrete, existential self with all my determinants.

What am I for? How will I know what I am to become? In the Exercises, we postulate that God our Creator and Lord has real, concrete hopes in us and for us. We postulate that we can know them in knowing our truest, most authentic desires. We come to be what God hopes us to be by enacting those desires in freedom. They are our desires; they are God's desires. So we cooperate with God in making our selves and, since our desires and gifts are important to it, in making our life world.

Plainly, discovering your authentic desires looms centrally important. During the Spiritual Exercises, you will let God teach you how your desires are shaped and often distorted by world, flesh, and evil. You stand solidly with the whole church and all the saints; you isolate and set aside what others have wanted of you and for you; you marginalize conventional yearning for security, plenty, and approval. Over and over again, you will present to God and beg Him for *lo que quiero*, what I want.

### The Principle of Active Indifference

To find out what you truly, authentically want to do with and in your life, and therefore what God hopes in you, is not simple. The strategy adopted in these Exercises requires that you adopt a difficult stance: You commit yourself at the start to put God first, before all else that you know and cherish. You want to place all things now in your life or to come into it — no matter how good and desirable — after God. No other absolute for you, no principle that forces choice, such as, You cannot be rich enough; or, Security first.

Instead, you will hold the stance that Ignatius calls "indifference." He does not mean diffidence or laziness or disinterest; he describes here a principle of action and even of strong desiring. It is something like this: When you first face some option — a career, a job, a friendship — you want above all to find what God hopes in you. You reject any predisposition or pre-judgment to one option over another. So, if you face an election of a state in life, you do not go into it with the principle in place that you will choose whatever leads to more money. Refusing to go one way or the other mindlessly or under external pressures, you choose instead to let your desires rise and clarify until the moment comes when you have a clear spiritual sense that *this particular desire* rises directly out of God's passionately creative love in you. And then you will know what you truly want and what God hopes in you.

# ✤  Ignatian Text  ✤

SPIRITUAL EXERCISES [21]
to gain mastery over one's self
and to live a well-ordered life
not making life choices
that take shape
from disordered affects

## Presupposition [22]

The one who gives the Exercises and the one who goes through them can insure that they will be better helped and get better results if they share this presupposition: Every good Christian is more ready to find a correct meaning in a neighbor's statement than to reject it as erroneous. If we cannot construe it in some orthodox sense, we ask how he meant it. If he meant to say something wrong, then we try to correct him, moved by love. If this is not good enough, then we try every feasible way to bring our neighbor to some correct meaning in the statement so as to save it.

## Principle and Foundation [23]

Each living person is created to praise, revere, and serve God our Lord and in doing that, to save himself.

All the other beings on the face of the earth are created for the sake of humankind, to help each person realize the original purpose he is created to achieve.

From this it follows that as far as things further his original purpose, so far a person uses them; as far as things hinder his original purpose, so far a person avoids them.

To achieve this, we ought to keep ourselves indifferent to all created things that are left to our free choice and are not forbidden. It comes to this, that we do not seek in our own self-interest health rather than sickness, wealth rather than penury, honor rather than contempt, a long life rather than a short one, and so on for everything else.

We desire and choose solely on the grounds of what contributes more to realizing the original purpose for which we are created.

# First Week

===✛===

✛ **Comment 5** ✛

# The Work of the First Week

You have been praying now for two, three, or perhaps five days. As Ignatius had to do, you have been correcting a deep error in the human spirit about God's work in the world. We tend to make this the model of God's work: sin and then redemption, making the initiative rise out of our sin. We have to learn that God's creative love comes first, and not our sins. The true model of God's work in the world is creation and salvation, all of it God's initiative.

During the early days of the Exercises, even if you had been praying regularly for some time, you tested out your image of God. You may have been worshiping a god of blazing anger rather than the Father of all consolations; a calculating, punitive god rather than the Giver of every good gift. Not many of us are easy with a God who claims to be like a mother suckling her infant, like a father stooping to feed his child, or a hen collecting chicks under her wing.

As they pray through the First Week, exercitants often realize in anguish that they have long considered God as Taskmaster, Uncaring Parent, or Angry Avenger. Ignatius began this way himself. Early on, during the first months of his repentance, he could not find enough ways to enact his self-hatred (the expression is his own). He suffered mental agony close to madness from scruples, assigning to himself a Bookkeeper God who relentlessly sniffed out sin.

You may come to see, helped by insights of depth psychology, how the sinful structures that you absorbed in your family relationships profoundly affect your relationship with God. One son abandoned as a teenager by his father had to beg in anguish that he might never again believe that God could hate him. A woman full of resentments from rearing by cold parents could barely come to believe that God cared in the least about her thoughts and actions.

As you accept the true God as your God, you deepen your ability to accept yourself as you are — not as you might have been, or could become, or ought to be. You say yes to the self God is creating you. You accept God's acceptance of you, and this brings with it a deep gratitude to God.

Gratitude is the key to this prayer on sin, as Ignatius indicates in one of the few exuberant paragraphs in his whole text, the fifth point of the second Exercise [60]. Ignatius once wrote in a letter that every sin is at root the sin of ingratitude. Not everyone is given the gift to grasp that, or accepts the gift given. You will find the full grace of the Exercises only if you grow to this deep sense of gratitude, the sense of receiving everything from God and of being yourself a gift, and the correlative sense of both owing everything to God and wanting keenly to return all to God. "It's really a tremendous, joyful thing, when you think about it," one exercitant said while weeping over his sins and sinfulness.

## The Structures of Sin

The First Week of the Spiritual Exercises draws you to experience sin as you have introjected it into yourself and also as it has marred every relationship among humankind and still does. Ignatius's exercitants would have experienced sin as an arrogant rupture of God's perfect ordering and a deliberate rejection of God's courteous but mighty governance. You are more likely to experience sin as a damage or a break in your relationship with God, then with others and with your life world, and even in your relationship with yourself (how you see yourself, appreciate yourself, treat yourself).

You will also be helped by the current stress on the "structures of sin." Today we have grown keenly aware of how ghettoes, peer pressures, excess of wealth or of need, and so on, make evil more available to some than to others and seem almost to drive some inescapably into evil. You may yourself have been the victim of some of the abuses that now seem structured into family systems.

Remembering, examining, detailing your sins and sinfulness might promise to fill you with desolation and even despair. It drove Francis Xavier to go without food or drink for days, as it has done exercitants today. They feel their self-betrayal to the marrow of their bones. They burn in shame, disappointed at how miserably they have missed their mark or fallen short of the standard their own spirits set for themselves.

If you focus on your own sin too much, however, you can make yourself suffer greatly during these days. One person kept saying of a sin, near despair, "It is *me!*" Others are not so foolish, but some weep in frustration that they cannot rid themselves of some habit of sin. Others suffer because they will not accept that they are making impossible demands on themselves that God neither makes nor condones. All such people will keep on suffering until they shift their focus off their sinful selves and onto their loving, merciful God. These lessons come hard, and the prayer of the First Week is often arduous.

This intense prayer on sin, however, does not in the least resemble a neurotic episode. You separate out moral shame and guilt from neurotic shame and guilt. You have sinned before God, who alone knows the measure of your guilt. Your self-examination and the memory of your sins may indeed evoke self-excoriation and self-loathing. Your meditations on sin in the world will bring you a profound sense of humankind's powerlessness in the face of even its own evil. But these appreciations come in God's presence, who will not let you see into the horror of sin until He has taught you how He loves you, and then only in the measure in which you have accepted your Lord's love.

God's love is incarnate, and from the first time you approach God to speak after you have considered sin, you stand beneath the cross and speak with Jesus hanging there. You do this not to torture yourself; you do it to make certain you know how great is Jesus Christ's love for you and for humankind.

Ordinarily, as you appreciate the ugliness of your and your world's sin, you abandon your exile and allow God to fill you with gratitude. What was guilt and unbearable transmutes into what is thanks, and a yes, and weighty joy. You comprehend how the church can sing about the sin of Adam and Eve, "Oh, happy fault that drew down into our humanness such a Savior!"

✤ **Comment 6** ✤

# The Beginning Exercises

The materials of the First Week are in three distinct parts. The first set of texts [24–44] introduces methods of examining your conscience and your life. These Ignatius referred to as "the easier exercises" that he gave to beginners.

The second set of texts [45–72] lays out the material for the five hours of prayer you go through each day during the First Week. The third set of texts [73–90] offers a set of additional notes that frame what is called "Ignatian contemplation," and summarizes the church's wisdom on the use of physical penances.

### Self-examination and the Sacrament of Reconciliation

When Ignatius first began helping someone, he would urge the use of the "Examen of Conscience." He brought out this method to help as many people as possible, people whom he could not or would not invite through the rest of the Exercises. Keep in mind that in Manresa and Vicenza and in inner-city Paris and Rome, he was teaching the Ten Commandments and the Seven Deadly Sins to people who had had virtually no religious instruction and who rarely heard preaching. Today this kind of instruction is less necessary. Even so, while directors of weekend preached retreats talk a dozen times on the materials of all four Weeks, they actually aim to bring people to examine their lives.

Ignatius developed his own way of examining himself during the first weeks and months after his conversion. Late in his life, a close associate said, he still examined his actions and intentions every day, assiduously comparing today with yesterday, this week with last, this year with the past year. The texts in the *Spiritual Exercises*, then, grew out of his own practices and out of his experiments to "help souls" from his earliest days in Manresa.

Ignatius, reared in a culture framed in periodical days and seasons of penance, did not have to invent much in these texts. He had access to small books called "penitentials," which listed sins and vices and detailed ways of examining his conscience and preparing for the Sacrament of Penance. Obviously, to take one instance, Ignatius's division of sins into thoughts, words, and deeds is no more original than his division of words into letters. He did do something original, however, in taking a diffused tradition and focusing it into a brief exercise and a systematic way of growing out of weaknesses and failings. His five points have become fairly standard throughout the church and continue to be used.

The first exercise, "Daily Particular Examen," helps to change habits of sin by focusing your attention on one particular action or omission. The exercise aims at what you do or do not do. It addresses only indirectly how you feel about your habit and how it shapes your feelings about yourself.

Today we have difficulty focusing exclusively on a deed done, tending to consider inclusively the person acting, subconscious motivations, the context, and so on. To us, therefore, this exercise can seem voluntaristic and mechanical, an almost Pelagian way of making ourselves holy. We might remember that Benjamin Franklin, a thorough rationalist, used a method like this for self-improvement. Yet this particular method and even those in "Four Additions" [27] are not so different from carefully crafted practices taught in journaling workshops and in human potential movements.

In point of fact, directors today do not seem to put much stress on the details. They stress, rather, a careful reflection on the way things stand between you and God, emphatically beginning with the first point of recognizing the gifts of this time so as to recall gratitude to God. During the Exercises, you make this reflection at noon and at night, focusing on how well you are doing what you set out to do [90]. Directors hope that you will make it daily for the rest of your life.

## The Start of Discerning Spirits

The second text is "General Examen of Conscience" [32–43]. Ignatius records here the concrete doctrine about grave and venial sin that he was teaching people at Manresa and Salamanca and that caught the attention of the Inquisition. He was teaching nothing outside of the ordinary doctrine of the church, and he cites verbatim at one point the theology he copied down from Ludolph's *Life of Christ*.

In this text, Ignatius raises the church's belief that some of your thoughts rise from outside yourself, from spirits [32]. You need to note right here the firm postmodern belief that individuals have thoughts that come from outside themselves. We say without hesitation that women and men are moved by team spirit or war fever, and we give epochs titles like "The Era of Good Feeling."

Of course, Ignatius thought of these spirits as personified; you may tend to think of them as forces or movements. It is hard to know which belief causes greater anxiety, but we can be as responsible as was Ignatius about the spirit we follow. If you believe in impersonal movements and psychosocial influences, for instance, you face the responsibility of choosing your environment, your reading and viewing, your friendships, and a great deal else in this land of hidden persuaders.

## The General Confession

Following his own advice about praising the Sacrament of Reconciliation along with the church [354], Ignatius urged its use in the *Spiritual Exercises* [18, 19, 32, 44, 326]. He used to urge people to confess often, at a time when the sacrament was coming under a severe attack led by John Calvin.

He was following church law. Since at least the tenth century, the church had been requiring that all believers receive Communion at Easter time. The Fourth Lateran Council had reflected on this Paschal Communion and declared that if you have committed a grave sin during the year, then you are also obliged to go to confession. You would then make what is thought of as a necessary general confession. You might note that exercitants who make a necessary general confession, as some do, are in effect turning away from a sinful life.

Well before Ignatius's day, however, Christians were making the general confession not because it was necessary, but freely and because they chose to. Ignatius made such a confession during Holy Week when the Companions elected him general. In the centuries since then, devout people have developed this practice, and many people who lead an interior life make an annual general confession. They commonly make this general confession out of devotion during their annual retreat.

Ignatius adverts to both kinds of general confession here, necessary and done out of devotion, suggesting to those going through all the Exercises of the First Week that they make the confession at its end [44]. Your director will almost surely urge you to make a general confession and will probably suggest, if he is a priest, that you might want to confess to someone else. This is ancient Jesuit practice, perhaps related to the fact that Ignatius, almost all the years that he was teaching and directing these Spiritual Exercises, did it as a layman.

Your director, however, will point out that this confession is not the purpose of the First Week. Its purposes are to grieve over the sadness of sin in the world, to feel shame and sorrow for your own sin and revulsion from its disorders in your spirit, and to accept God's merciful love by determining how to serve God instead of sin in what future is given to you.

## ✤ Ignatian Text ✤

# Daily Particular Examen [24]

*This includes each day three occasions and two self-examinations.*

First, in the morning. When he wakes up, he ought to set himself to watch alertly against the particular sin or failing that he wants to get rid of or to amend.

Second, after the midday meal. He ought to ask God for what [25] he wants, which here is the grace to remember how many times he has fallen into the particular sin or failing and to avoid it from now on.

Then he promptly makes the first Examen. He makes himself take stock of the particular thing he has set himself to correct or amend by going through the day hour by hour or by other blocks of time from the moment he woke up to the Examen. Then he ought to mark on the top line of the D══════ a dot for each time he has fallen into that sin or failing. That done, he determines once again to improve until the second Examen he will make.

[26]     Third, after the evening meal. He ought to make a second Examen, hour by hour the way he did earlier, starting after the first Examen and coming down to the second. Then he ought to mark on the bottom line of the D══════ a dot for each time he has fallen into that sin or failing.

## [27] Four Additions

*These four Additions will help to get rid of a particular sin or failing more quickly.*

First Addition: Each time he falls into that particular sin or defect, he might put his hand to his heart, feeling sorry that he has fallen. He can do this even in a crowd without having anyone notice.

[28]     Second Addition: The first line of the D══════ records the first Examen and the second line, the second Examen. So, in the evening he ought to see whether he has made any improvement from the first line to the second, that is, from the first Examen to the second.

[29]     Third Addition: He can then compare the second day with the first, that is, the two Examens today with the two he made yesterday, to see whether he is making any improvement from one day to the next.

[30]     Fourth Addition: He can then compare one week with another, to see whether he has made any improvement this week over last week.

[31]     Note. The first D══════, a capital, stands for the Lord's Day; the second, a smaller letter, stands for Monday; the third for Tuesday, and so on.

## General Examen of Conscience [32]

*This is to purify the self, and to help make better confessions.*

I take it as given that three kinds of thoughts occur to me: One kind comes from my own freedom and desiring and is entirely my own. The other two kinds come from outside of myself, one from a good spirit and one from an evil spirit.

### *Concerning Thoughts* [33]

There are two meritorious ways of handling evil thoughts that come from outside of myself:

First, when a thought that I commit a mortal sin occurs to me, I immediately react against it and effectively quash it.

Second meritorious handling: The same evil thought comes to [34] me and I react against it. Then it keeps coming back to me over and over again. And I keep on reacting to it and in the end effectively quash it. This second way is more meritorious than the first.

A person sins venially when that same thought to commit a [35] mortal sin arises and he entertains it, dwelling on it for a while, or taking some sensual pleasure from it, or reacting against it somewhat casually.

There are two ways of sinning mortally: [36]

First, a person consents to an evil thought, determined to act out later what he consented to, or determined to act it out if he can.

Second, a person actually does the sinful act consented to. This [37] sin is greater for three reasons: First, it endures longer; second, it is more intense; third, it does greater harm to the two persons.

[38] *Concerning Words*

It is never good to swear by the Creator or by any creature except according to the truth, under necessity, and with reverence.

Necessity: There is no necessity when a person just chooses to affirm some statement or other by an oath. Necessity means that the statement has some important bearing on the welfare of the person's self or of his body, or on his temporal interests.

Reverence: This means that a person thinks carefully before he uses the name of his Creator and Lord, and shows the honor and reverence owed to God.

[39] It must be said that we sin more grievously when we swear by the Creator wantonly than when we swear wantonly by some creature.

Yet it is more difficult to swear as we ought — according to the truth, under necessity, and with reverence — when we swear by some creature than when we swear by the Creator. Here are some reasons.

First, when we want to swear by some creature: The desire to swear by a creature does not make us feel as nicely careful about telling the truth or having to swear to it as does the desire to swear by the Creator and Lord of all creatures.

Second, when we do swear by some creature, we do not find it as easy to maintain reverence and respect for the Creator as when we swear by and name that same Creator and Lord. For the intention to name God our Lord carries with it deeper affects of respect and reverence than the intention to name some creature.

Because of this, it is more permissible for the spiritually mature to swear by some creature than it is for the spiritually immature. For the mature, through constant contemplation and the enlightenment of their understanding, are more likely to consider, meditate, and contemplate how God our Lord is in each creature according to His own essence, presence, and power. As a consequence, when they swear by a creature they are more likely to be disposed to show respect and give homage to their Creator and Lord than are the immature.

Third, constant swearing by creatures runs the risk of idolatry — more in the spiritually immature than in the mature.

[40] It is not good to talk idly. I take talk to be idle that does not profit me or anyone else, and was not meant to. Considered this

way, no talk is idle that helps or is intended to help the speaker himself or someone else, or to help their physical well-being or belongings. They would not be idle words even when a person is talking about something foreign to his own state in life, for example, when a religious talks about war or business. Hence, there is merit in anything said for a good purpose; there is sin in anything said for an evil purpose, or to no purpose at all.

We should not defame another person or spread talk about [41] him. For if I make public another's mortal sin that has been hidden, I sin mortally; if another's hidden venial sin, I sin venially; if another's defect, I broadcast my own defect.

However, as long as we mean well, we can speak of the sin or failing of another in two ways:

First, when the sin is publicly known, as in the case of a known prostitute, or of a conviction in a trial, or of a public error infecting those we dwell among.

Second, when one person tells the secret sin of a sinner to another person who, it is hoped, can help the sinner rise from his sin. Plainly, the one who tells must expect, with some good reason, that this other person can help the sinner.

*Concerning Deeds* [42]

The Ten Commandments, the laws of the church, and the ordinances of superiors form the frame for judging our deeds. Whatever deed transgresses any of these is sinful, more seriously or less depending on what it transgresses.

About the ordinances of superiors: I mean things like the indults and indulgences connected with crusades, for example, or those granted to deeds done for peace on condition of confession and Communion. One sins more than slightly when he acts against superiors' ordinances and their exhortations to do good, or leads others to do so in these matters.

## Method of Making the General Examen of Conscience [43]

*This includes five points.*

1. The first point is to thank God our Lord for all the good things I have received.

2. The second point is to ask for the gift of recognizing my sins and of getting rid of them.

3. The third point is to demand an account of myself from the time I woke up to the Examen, going hour by hour, or taking successive blocks of time. I examine thoughts first, then words, then deeds, following the order given in the Particular Examen.

4. The fourth point is to beg God's pardon for my failures.

5. The fifth point is to determine to amend, by the grace of God.

I say the Our Father.

## [44] General Confession and Communion

When an exercitant freely chooses to make a general confession at this point, he will find among many other advantages these three special ones:

1. First, even though someone who confesses every year would not be obliged to make a general confession, he will advance more and gain more merit. For he feels at this juncture deeper sorrow over all of the sins and perverseness in his whole life.

2. Second, during the Spiritual Exercises, a person comes to a more intimate interior knowledge of sins and of their viciousness than he can during times when he does not give such attention to his interior life. So, reaching now a deeper knowledge and sharper sorrow for his own sins, he will draw more profit and gain more merit from a general confession than he might have before this.

3. Third, as a consequence of having made a better confession and come to better spiritual condition, he will find himself better disposed for the Most Blessed Sacrament and readier to receive. And this sacrament will not only strengthen him against falling into sin, but will keep him growing in grace.

It is better to make this general confession right after the Exercises of the First Week.

## ❖ Comment 7 ❖

# Meditating on Sin and Sinfulness

You have finished the preparatory days that you needed to begin your long retreat, perhaps three or four. In the Exercises at home, you have moved into the second month. During this time, your director will have introduced you to the Examens, and you will continue using that Exercise noon and night from now on.

Now you move into the meditations and contemplations that make up the First Week.

In the thirty-day retreat, you will pray five times a day. Each midnight, you will consider the paradigmatic mortal sins: of the angels, of the first humans, and of a person who chose to destroy herself or himself by a life of sin. Each morning, you will remember your own sins. Later in the morning, you will take up these two meditations again, adding a special prayer to the Lady Mary, the Lord Jesus, and to God the Father. Some time in the afternoon, you go through these matters once again, ending with that same Triple Colloquy. And finally, late each day, you will let the reality of Hell enlarge your grasp of the force of evil in any sin.

The way of praying introduced in this First Week, which Ignatius consistently calls "meditation," he found in the books he read and reread during his convalescence. Meditation had been practiced, however, since the psalmist "pondered God's law day and night." In the American classical philosophical tradition, this might be called "musing" or "musement." It is a matter of thinking things through, of weighing their meaning and import. You may also find yourself "contemplating," imagining the events of the angels' lightning fall or a person's slow descent into hate, and then relating what you have envisioned to your own complicity in sin.

### The Subject Matters for the Hours

In suggesting ways to consider the sin of the angels and of the first humans [45], which you do at midnight, your director is very likely to recommend some Scripture passages. We are today considerably more oriented toward the text of Scripture than were Ignatius's contemporaries. So you might ponder what Jesus said about the angels, "I watched Satan fall like lightning from heaven" (Luke 10:18); or the belief of the early church, "When the angels sinned, God imprisoned them" (2 Pet. 2:4). The sin of Adam and Eve [51], of course, you read about in Genesis. Perhaps you will use some of Paul's formulations: "Well then, sin entered the world through one man, and through sin death, and thus death has spread through the whole human race because everyone has sinned" (Rom. 5:12).

Ignatius also asks you to consider in this first hour of prayer, as a way of understanding what sin is and does and of coming to a proper fear of it, the sin of a person who has been condemned for a "single sin." You need to know that this does not necessarily mean a single act. Ignatius and his times were deeply impressed that persons could do a single act and ruin themselves, but they knew that you have to build up to such an act. They saw patterns in that deadly buildup that they called the seven Capital Sins, and Ignatius had in mind a person ruined by one of those seven sins. You will probably do better to ponder how a string of sins — little lies, small thefts, casual use of others carnally — becomes a way of sinfulness and then a life of sin. It follows its own laws and grows lethal to the sinner and to those around.

These materials — angels, Adam and Eve, a lost sinner — you cover in the hour of prayer at midnight. You may or may not go through all of them in one midnight, but whether you do or not, you will always find some good when you go back to them on other midnights. You are begging God to let you grasp the disorder in humanity and in our life world caused by humankind's sins. You need God's gift: Sin itself is a mystery.

In the second hour of prayer in the early morning, you reflect directly on the sins you have committed throughout your life [55]. How you review your sins and sinfulness is a very personal thing, but Ignatius suggests a specific method, and you are likely to find good in at least parts of it. You need to remember that the Exercise is not mainly a detailed examination of conscience; you are making a meditation on the history of a unique relationship, your sinning and God's mercifully loving. You are begging God to let you know the disorder in your own self, and even in your life world, caused by your personal sins.

In the third hour of prayer, later in the morning, you simply go back over what you have prayed on, sometimes finishing the matters you have not yet prayed on. Ignatius calls this a "repetition" [62]. To prepare for it, you need your notes to find those places in earlier hours of prayer where you found good and those places where you found emptiness or darkness. You may have been moved to tears that some genuinely evil habit did not ruin your life as it might have; you go back to the light and the fervor and deepen yourself in it. Or again, you may have been moved not one inch by the thought of a person destroyed forever by sin; you take up the thought again and ask why you are unmoved by a thought that moved Jesus deeply. You end this hour and the one following with what Ignatius calls the "Triple Colloquy," mentioned already, in which you address the Lady Mary, Jesus your Savior, and the Father.

The fourth hour entails more repetition [64], which you quickly learn characterizes Ignatian spirituality and the Exercises. This repetition is a different kind, however. Instead of choosing individual points to go back to, you think steadily through all that you have prayed on, moving through your reflections on angels, Adam and Eve, a single lost person, and your own sins and sinfulness. You end this very characteristic Ignatian exercise, which he calls a "summary," with the Triple Colloquy.

Finally, you will spend an hour at the end of each day, or at the end of each week in the Exercises in daily life, meditating on Hell. The exercitant in Ignatius's day had no trouble at all with this meditation; Hell was a vivid and dire threat, felt by many as intensely as Martin Luther felt it. Some few exercitants today find their faith confused by recent theological speculations, but for almost all of us, Scripture rings with conviction. You might take the Last Judgment in Matthew 25 or the parable of Lazarus and Dives, and find echoing in your spirit the admonition of the fierce rabbi from Nazareth recorded in Luke 12, "Do not be afraid of those who kill the body and after that can do no more. Fear him who, after he has killed, has the power to cast into Hell."

## Three Ignatian Practices

The first of three particular practices that you will adopt during these days is the first Prelude [47]. You have heard discussions of "centering," a way of recollecting yourself or coming to self-concentration. In some traditions, you draw into yourself and withdraw from all else; in others, you concentrate on a pebble or a candle. In the Exercises, you recollect yourself or come to self-concentration by imagining yourself in a chosen place. Later on, for instance, you will make your "composition of place," in Bethlehem or on Calvary. This is the distinctively Ignatian act of centering, or self-concentration.

During this First Week, Ignatius recommends that you compose yourself in the world poisoned with the radioactivity of sin and peopled with women and men completely given to disordered lives. He uses an image that few of us would find instructive or moving: the soul exiled among brute beasts. You need to remember that Ignatius shared the images of the human condition that informed the work of his contemporaries, the tortured woodcarvings of Albrecht Dürer, for instance, and Michelangelo's "Last Judgment" (being painted while Ignatius's book was being examined in the Vatican). You might get some inkling of how they felt the human self in its life world if you imagine yourself incarcerated in the infamous Gulag Archipelago, mental hospitals turned into halls of mental torture. Later first Preludes are considerably simpler.

The second practice, which you may already have used in the preparation days, is the Colloquy [53, 63]. Though you freely talk with God any time while meditating, you always make a Colloquy at the end of the hour. Ignatius recommends doing this during the First Week in two ways of his own inventing. In the first, you stand under the cross of Jesus pondering how He came there and asking yourself three questions [53]. In the other, the Triple Colloquy already mentioned, you beg for specific gifts through Our Lady, from our Lord Jesus Christ, and from the Father [63].

The third practice helps with the continuity of your experience: the Review of Prayer [77]. After you have finished your hour of prayer, you spend about fifteen minutes remembering what you thought about and prayed over. You are doing a different exercise, in which you investigate how the hour went: long and boring or fast and full, teeming with ideas or charged with affects. You jot into a notebook what you find, particularly of developing desires and decisions. Ignatius, who wanted to remember every gift given by God, urges the importance of this Exercise, and current experience confirms it, particularly if you face the election of a way of life or some other serious choices.

## ✤ Ignatian Text ✤

# The Meditations of the First Week

### First Exercise [45]

*This meditation turns the memory, understanding, and free will toward the first, second, and third sins. It includes, besides the Readiness Prayer and two Preludes, three main points and a Colloquy.*

Readiness Prayer. The prayer for readiness is to beg God our [46] Lord for the grace that all my intentions, all my outward acts, all my inward operations, may be directed purely to the praise and service of His Divine Majesty.

First Prelude. I compose myself by imagining the place. [47]

Here something must be noted. When the contemplation or meditation deals with things that can be seen, for instance, when we are contemplating Christ our Lord, who can be seen, then the composition consists in seeing by the power of imagination the physical location where we find what we want to contemplate. I say the "physical location." I mean, for instance, a temple or a mountain where I might find Jesus or His mother — whatever fits the matter I wish to contemplate.

When the subject is nothing visible, as here in a meditation on sin, I will compose myself by using the power of imagination to envision my immortal spirit like a prisoner in this body that will decay, and my whole self — I mean, myself as inspirited flesh — like an exile in this dark valley among brute beasts.

Second Prelude. I beg God for what I want and desire. What [48] I ask for will depend on the subject matter. For instance, when I contemplate the Resurrection, I beg for joy with Christ full of joy.

When I contemplate the Passion, I beg grief, tears, and anguish with Christ anguished.

Here I will beg for shame and confusion about myself, as I see how many have been damned because of one mortal sin, and how many times, for how many sins, I have deserved to be damned forever.

[49] Note. Always, before every contemplation and meditation, these must be made: the Readiness Prayer, which never changes, and the two Preludes just mentioned, which change several times to match the subject matter.

[50] First Point. The first point is to focus my memory on the first sin, that of the angels; then my mind, thinking it through; then my free will, determining to remember and understand the whole event so that I will feel more full of shame and confusion. I compare the one sin of the angels to my many sins; they went to Hell, which I have deserved by my many sins, for one sin.

This would be to focus the memory on the sin of the angels: I recall that they were created in the state of grace. They did not want to use their freedom to give reverence and obedience to their Creator and Lord. They fell into pride and were transmuted from grace to malice. They were pitched out of heaven and down into Hell.

Then I use my understanding to work through all this in careful detail, and my free will to stir up deeper affects.

[51] Second Point. The second point is to use the same procedure, applying my three powers to the sin of Adam and Eve. I focus my memory on what long penance they did for this sin, and how deep a decadence spread through the whole human race, putting many people on the road to Hell.

This would be to focus on the second sin, that of our first parents: I recall that Adam was created on the Plain of Damascus and placed in an earthly Paradise. Eve was created from one of his ribs. They were forbidden to eat of the tree of knowledge, ate of it, and sinned in that. Afterward, clothed in garments made of animal hides, they were driven out of Paradise. So they lost their original justice, and they lived without it all their lives, laboring hard and doing great penance.

Then, again, I use my understanding to work through all this in careful detail, and I use my free will as indicated.

[52] Third Point. We do the same over again, taking a third sin,

which is the particular sin of someone who went to Hell because of a single mortal sin. Consider the many others, uncounted, damned for fewer sins than I have committed.

I say, do the same things over again for this third, particular sin. I remember the seriousness and malice of sin against our Creator and Lord. I apply my understanding, reasoning how by sinning and going against the infinite Goodness, the person truly merited being damned forever. And I end using my free will as indicated.

Colloquy. Imagining Christ right before you, hanging on the [53] cross, make a Colloquy. How is it that He has come from being Creator to making Himself human? How it is that He came from eternal life to death in time, and came so as to die for my sins? Turning it about, I ask of myself: What have I done for Christ? What am I doing for Christ? What ought I do for Christ?

And in this way, perceiving Him for who He is, and fixed thus to a cross, I talk through what comes into my mind.

Note. The Colloquy quite correctly goes on as a conversation, [54] as though one friend were speaking to another or a servant to his master, sometimes asking some grace, at other times blaming himself for some misdeed, at still others talking over his affairs and asking advice.

Then say the Our Father.

## Second Exercise [55]

*This meditation is on our sins. It includes, after the Readiness Prayer and the two Preludes, five points, and a Colloquy.*

Readiness Prayer. The Readiness Prayer will be the same.
First Prelude. The first Prelude, composing myself, will be the same.
Second Prelude. The second Prelude is to ask for what I want. Here I beg for intense and increasing sorrow and tears for my sins.
First Point. The first point is the indictment of my sins. I call [56] to mind all the sins of my life, remembering them year by year or period by period. Three recollections help this process: first, the location and the house where I lived; second, the associations I had with others; and third, my career at the time.
Second Point. The second point is to feel the weight of the sins. [57]

I muse on the loathsomeness and viciousness of every mortally sinful act in itself, even were it not forbidden.

[58]      Third Point. The third point is to consider who I am, humbling myself by making comparisons:

1.  Who am I compared with the whole of humankind?

2.  What are all living people compared with the angels and saints in paradise?

3.  I think, what is all of creation compared with God? Then of myself alone, what can I be?

4.  I consider all the corruption and loathsomeness of my body.

5.  I see myself like an ulcer or abscess; from me have issued so many sins and so much evil and such vile poison.

[59]      Fourth Point. The fourth point is to consider who God is, against whom I have sinned. I go through His attributes and contrast them with their contraries in myself: His wisdom and my ignorance, His omnipotence and my powerlessness, His justice and my iniquity, His goodness and my malice.

[60]      Fifth Point. The fifth point is a cry of wonder as, with deepening feelings, I wonder how it happened that every other creature let me keep living and preserved me in life? The angels: Since they are the sword of divine justice, how could they have put up with me, and guarded me, and prayed for me? The saints: Why have they kept interceding for me and asking favors for me? Then the heavens, sun, moon, stars, all the elements; fruits, birds, fish, animals: Why did they preserve me? Then the earth: How has it not opened up to swallow me, creating new Hells for me to be tormented in forever?

[61]      Colloquy. I conclude with a Colloquy on mercy, talking with and giving thanks to God our Lord for granting me life down to the present, and determining with His grace to amend in the future. I say the Our Father.

## [62] Third Exercise

*This is a repetition of the first and second Exercises, with three Colloquies.*

After the Readiness Prayer and the two Preludes, I go through the first and the second Exercises again. I identify the points in which I have felt deeper consolation or desolation or greater spiritual appreciation, and I dwell on them. After this, I make three Colloquies in the following manner:

First Colloquy. The first Colloquy is with Our Lady, that she [63] would obtain for me from her Son and Lord the grace of three gifts:

1. The first, that I might have a deep understanding of my sins from within, and feel revolted by them;

2. The second, that I might sense the disorder in the way I have been behaving, so that, repelled by it, I might correct my life and put order in it;

3. The third, that I might have insight into the world, so that I come to feel disdain for it all and put away from me everything that is vain and worldly.

At this point, I say the Hail Mary.

Second Colloquy. The second Colloquy is with the Son, asking that He obtain these same gifts for me from the Father.

After that, I say the Anima Christi.

Third Colloquy. The third Colloquy is with the Father, again going through the same gifts and asking that the Eternal Father Himself would grant them to me.

And I end with the Our Father.

### Fourth Exercise [64]

*This Exercise consists in making a summary of the third Exercise.*

I have said "making a summary" because with steady effort I set my mind to thinking through only things remembered from contemplation in the earlier exercises and do not let it wander onto other things. I also make the same three Colloquies.

### Fifth Exercise [65]

*This is a meditation on Hell. It includes, besides the Readiness Prayer and two Preludes, five points and a Colloquy.*

Readiness Prayer. The Readiness Prayer is the usual one.

First Prelude. The first Prelude is to compose myself in the place. Here I imagine I see with my own eyes the length, breadth, and depth of Hell.

Second Prelude. I beg God for what I want. Here I ask for an intimate sense of the punishment suffered by the damned, so that if my failures ever make me grow forgetful of the love of my eternal Lord, at least my fear of these punishments will keep me from falling into sin.

[66]     First Point. The first point will be to imagine seeing the great flames, and immortal spirits in them like bodies afire.

[67]     Second Point. The second point will be to imagine hearing with my own ears the wailing, the howling, the screams, and the blasphemies against Christ our Lord and against all His saints.

[68]     Third Point. The third point is to smell for myself the smoke, the sulphurous stench, the filth, and the rotten things.

[69]     Fourth Point. The fourth point is to taste the bitter things in my own mouth: the tears, the sadness, the worm of conscience.

[70]     Fifth Point. The fifth point is to feel on my own flesh the touch of the flames burning up the immortal spirits.

[71]     Colloquy. I make a Colloquy to Christ our Lord. I call to mind the immortal spirits who are in Hell, some because they did not believe in the coming of Christ and others because, though they believed, they did not live according to His commands. I divide them into three groups:

1. Those lost before His coming;

2. Those lost during His lifetime;

3. Those lost after His life on earth ended.

When I have done that, I give thanks to Christ our Lord that He has not let me fall into any of these three groups and end my life as they did.

I also give Him thanks that He has always until now shown me such kindness and mercy.

I finish by saying the Our Father.

[72]     Note. The first Exercise is to be made at midnight; the second, promptly on rising in the morning; the third, either before or after Mass, but before the midday meal; the fourth, around the time of Vespers; and the fifth, an hour before the evening meal.

I consider this pattern of prayer times, with some variations, the pattern for all four Weeks. Still, this depends on whether age, spiritual dispositions, and physical condition mean that the one going through the Exercises finds good in five times of prayer or in fewer.

✦ **Comment 8** ✦

# The Structure of Ignatian Meditation

As you continue praying five hours a day, or at home an hour every day week after week, you will be doing each of the hours in much the same way, having learned a set of practices from your director. Ignatius summarized these practices, which mark characteristically Ignatian prayer, in some instructions called the "Additions." In them he describes not only how to begin, continue, and conclude the hour of prayer; he also indicates some activities outside of the hour that deepen it and enliven it. He places here a cameo treatise on corporal penances, which people given to mental prayer consider integral to lifting the heart to God.

Occasionally an exercitant complains that these are rules and constrain freedom; certainly some exercitants already have a developed method in their prayer. But of themselves the Additions (like any proven method) no more constrain human liberty than the sonnet form constrained Shakespeare's poetry or the camera constrained Ansel Adams's eye. You are like an artist when you pray, hoping for and accepting inspiration and creating as you go. Understand, these directives give shape to *exercises;* they do not produce prayer any more than directions on a weight machine produce bulky muscles. Still, centuries of tradition in every religion have certified the usefulness to liberty of set procedures.

## The Ignatian Method

When you have learned to observe all of the Annotations and Additions, you will approach your hour in a way like this: You start by standing a few steps from your chair (or the blanket you will sit or lie on, or the kneeler you will kneel on), collecting yourself in God's presence. You offer to God everything you think and want during the coming hour, and indeed your whole self. This prayer, the Readiness Prayer, you neither omit nor change.

Then for a very brief moment you place the event you are about to consider into the whole sweep of salvation history. You might have recalled when praying about one person lost in Hell, for instance, that the whole salvation story begins again each time God creates life in a woman's womb. Perhaps later you will note that Jesus' baptism marks the end of God's work in secret and the beginning of God's work in public.

Recalling where a particular event fits into the whole of the salvation story also places you in that story. You find it quite natural then to concentrate for a moment on the physical place where the event took place. You compose yourself in that place, feeling the bitter loneliness of the damned person or the heat of the desert where Jesus is tempted.

In that place, you ask God for the gift or grace you want at this time. In Ignatian spiritual writing, this is often referred to as "the grace of the Week." This request is crucial, opening you to the action of the Spirit and orienting you within that action. All during the First Week, you composed yourself in the concrete chaos of your life world and there begged God for an intimate knowledge of sin's disorder and decay. If God revealed the mystery of iniquity to you and you wept with sorrow and dismay, then you had already opened yourself to that gift by your prayer of petition.

During the Second Week, you will beg God repeatedly to know, love, and follow Jesus of Nazareth. Why ask for this or for any such grace? Well, you cannot create in yourself the knowledge of Christ Jesus that saves. You cannot create a love for One whom you have never seen. However, neither could you accept that knowledge and that love unless you had committed yourself freely beforehand to say yes when God creates them in you.

### The Prayer for "What I Want"

It must be plain why Ignatius used the expression "what I want" more than any other in the *Spiritual Exercises*. In Ignatian spirituality, this is the radical way each unique creature cooperates with the Creator: desiring. Does it make sense, then, for all of us to ask for the same thing, directed by the author of a book? Well, you might say the same prayer as everyone else, but the fact is, you will not be begging merely a different piece of the same bread.

You come to mean concrete things by the plea, for instance, "to know Jesus," things unique to your unique self. Does every couple share the same love in marriage? Neither do you ask the same grace in this prayer. Rather, you are pursuing the goal of the Spiritual Exercises to discover and enact what you most authentically desire.

### Moving into Contemplation

This rather thorough orienting — being present to God, recalling salvation history, composing yourself in a place, asking God for the grace you want — is meant to take up only a few minutes. Then you move into the contemplation. You will already have selected for prayer certain words, notions, and images. This preparation distinguishes the contemplation of the Spiritual Exercises from other kinds of contemplation, particularly those calling on you to empty your mind and memory. The preparation also separates Ignatian contemplation from Benedictine *lectio divina*, in which as a rule you simply take a passage in Scripture and begin reading, to pause, meditate, and contemplate on whatever draws you. In the Exercises, you have chosen matters and materials beforehand, or your director has suggested a few notions about any Scripture passage you are to pray with. The traditional word for those few notions is "points," a rhetorical term still in use (you make several points in an address, for instance).

A few directors today hesitate to give points. They fear they might impinge on your freedom, or stand in the way of the Spirit. But many experienced directors note that points no more restrain freedom than steel netting around a tropical beach to fend off sharks restrains swimmers. The most experienced directors do not hesitate to give points (briefly, following Annotation 2), imitating

Ignatius. Others before him had suggested points for prayer, but Ignatius gave points precisely as a way of directing the exercitant. He considered the matter important enough to gather into one document the points that he had found useful [261–312].

During prayer itself, several dynamics promote openness to the Spirit of God and a couple close you down. You are more open when you are praying with your whole self, which might entail keeping food and drink discipline, darkening or decorating your room, and holding one posture as long as you are praying well or changing positions to pray better [76, 82, 79]. You find yourself closed down when you give in to a sense that you need to hurry through the material, so that you move from point to point as though you were preparing for an examination [76], or do nothing outside the time of prayer to sustain it from hour to hour.

After you have finished each hour of prayer with a Colloquy and (unless another prayer fits better) an Our Father, you do another typical Ignatian exercise, the "Review of Prayer," already mentioned [77]. With this done, you have completed the format of what is called "Ignatian contemplation." Keep in mind that these are the externals, no more the life of contemplation than a tortoise's shell is its life.

## About Corporal Penances

In a culture marked by both hedonism and narcissism, we find it hard to make sense of prescribed or even freely embraced corporal austerities like fasting. They seem to us part of alien cultures like those of the lamaseries in Nepal. Yet, we readily inflict pain on ourselves for the sake of our self-esteem or fame and position. Women willingly live on celery and endure harsh relations; men willingly grunt through weight machines and develop ulcers from work tensions.

Serious creative human endeavor in any culture elicits self-discipline and self-sacrifice. Canadian and Soviet athletes work an iron regimen that becomes the core of their lives. Japanese and American musicians practice laboriously by the hour, day after day. All over the earth, scientists, diplomats, and writers eschew leisure and skip food.

In somewhat the same way — though not exactly — people in all cultures who enter the serious quest for spiritual integrity and for a mature knowledge of God practice self-restraint and self-sacrifice. Buddhism, Hinduism, and animism draw their votaries into corporal penances, some of them, when fueled by enthusiasm, tinged with savagery.

The church's tradition reaches back to Jesus' own life and beyond that into the life of the People of God. Fasting, keeping long silences, postponing play and laughter, avoiding certain foods or drinks for life or for a time, even stinging the flesh with cords or rough clothing — these practices all come down to the church from the People's practice through thousands of years, certified by Jesus in His own life.

Some few have felt called by God to practice extreme physical penances, their interior freedom requiring this of them. They are the Olympic athletes of the interior life. Like Olympians, they are looked up to as somehow the ideal or the model. They themselves warn us to watch what we look up to and take as an ideal. Ignatius was such an Olympian, remember, walking barefoot through the cold, going ungroomed and unkempt, refusing meat and wine, and punishing his flesh with scourges and cords. He learned penances' value and the limits we need to place on them.

Ignatius's exact intention in these Norms was to temper eager people's corporal penances. His brief paragraphs can nonetheless be read as reminder of the great tradition of the People of God and of the church, and of the One who went into His own desert.

✢ **Ignatian Text** ✢

# Additions [73]

*These directives will help a person make the Exercises better and find what he wants more readily.*

First Addition. After I have gone to bed, while waiting to fall asleep, I think for as long as it takes to say the Hail Mary about when I will get up and why. I briefly sum up the Exercise I am to make.

[74]     Second Addition. When I first wake up, I do not let random thoughts into my mind but promptly focus my attention on what I am going to contemplate in the first Exercise in the middle of the night. By thinking of examples, I stir feelings of shame over the many sins I have committed. For instance, I picture a knight who finds himself standing before his king and the whole court, ashamed and confounded because he has gravely offended the lord from whom he had received many gifts and kindnesses in the past.

Or again, before the second Exercise, I account myself a great sinner. I think of myself as loaded down with fetters, by which I mean that I am bound up in chains and on my way to appear before the supreme, eternal Judge. I compare this with the way prisoners, chained and looking forward to the death sentence, go to face their temporal judge.

So I get dressed, keeping my mind focused on these thoughts or on others that are appropriate to the matter of the coming meditation.

[75]     Third Addition. I stand one or two steps away from the place where I am about to contemplate or meditate. For about as long as it takes to say the Our Father, I raise my mind on high and consider how God our Lord gazes down on me, and so on. Then I make a gesture of reverence and humility.

[76]     Fourth Addition. I enter into the contemplation, sometimes kneeling, sometimes lying prostrate on the floor, or lying on my back facing upward, or sitting, or standing, shifting only in search of what I want. We can note two things:

1. If I am finding what I want while on my knees, I do not change; and the same holds if I am lying prostrate on the floor, and so on.

2. If I am finding what I want in meditating on a particular point, I will not be anxious to move along, but will remain quietly on that point until I am satisfied.

[77]     Fifth Addition. For a quarter of an hour after I have finished an Exercise, sitting down or strolling about, I will consider how I have succeeded in the contemplation or meditation. If I have done

poorly, I will search for the reason why, and when I can find it, I will feel sorry and determined to do better another time. If I have done well, I will give thanks to God our Lord and continue next time in the same way.

Sixth Addition. I will choose not to think of what brings plea- [78] sure or joy, such as heavenly glory, the Resurrection, and so on. For any musing on delight and happiness will get in the way of what I want to feel, which is pain, sorrow, and tears for my sins. Hence, to keep fresh my desire to sorrow and to feel the pain, I do better to call to mind death and judgment.

Seventh Addition. For this same reason, I deprive myself of [79] brightness, shutting the blinds and the doors while I am in my room, except when I need light to recite the office, to read, or to eat.

Eighth Addition. I will not laugh or say things that provoke [80] laughter.

Ninth Addition. I will restrain my sight, looking up only to [81] receive or to say goodbye to someone with whom I have to talk.

Tenth Addition. This deals with penance. Penance is distin- [82] guished as interior or exterior. Interior penance consists in grieving over one's sins and in firmly resolving to commit neither them again nor any others. Out of this grows exterior penance, which consists in punishing ourselves for the sins we have committed. We inflict penances on ourselves in three principal ways:

1. The first way has to do with eating. Notice first that when we [83] fast from foods we never did need, we are practicing temperance, not penance. We do penance when we cut back even on what is good for us. As we cut back more and more, we do greater and stronger penance. Only, we are not to damage our constitution or make ourselves seriously ill.

2. The second way has to do with our sleeping habits. Here [84] again, it is no penance to rid ourselves of unnecessarily nice or sensuous arrangements. It is penance, though, when we take away something from the sleep we find convenient. The more we take away, the better the penance. Again, we are not to damage our constitution or make ourselves seriously ill. Nor should we deprive ourselves of a normal amount of sleep, unless we have a chronic habit of sleeping too much and we are trying to reach a reasonable mean.

3. The third way is to chastise the flesh by inflicting sensible [85]

pain on it. A person does this by wearing hair shirts, cords, or iron chains on his bare flesh, by scourging himself, or wounding himself, and by other kinds of austerities.

[86]     Note. In doing penances, it seems more fitting and safer that the pain be felt in the flesh and not penetrate down to the bone, so that it brings suffering but not sickness. Following this reasoning, it would appear more suitable to scourge oneself with thin cords that inflict pain through the skin than to do it some other way that inflicts serious internal injury.

[87]     Note I. The first note is that external penances are performed mainly to achieve these three things:

1.  To make satisfaction for past sins;

2.  To gain self-mastery. This means that sensual appetites are governed by reason and all lower faculties are better organized under higher faculties;

3.  To seek and find some grace or gift that he yearns to have. For instance, a person may be seeking to have a deep sorrow because of his sins, or because of the sufferings and sorrows which Christ our Lord went through in His Passion. Another person may be seeking the resolution of some doubt that he is suffering.

[88]     Note II. The second thing to note is that the First and the Second Additions ought to be observed for the Exercises at midnight and on rising in the morning and do not apply to those done at other times. The Fourth Addition should never be observed in church in front of other people, but only in a private place like the home.

[89]     Note III. When the person going through the Exercises keeps failing to find what he seeks — tears, consolations, and so on — it is often useful to make changes in his eating, sleeping, and other ways of doing penance. He could shift after doing penances for two or three days to doing none for two or three. One consideration is that some people do better with more penance and some people with less. Furthermore, we sometimes quit doing penance because of a tender love for our bodies and because of our erroneous decision that the human constitution cannot go through it and escape serious sickness; and on the other hand, we sometimes do too much penance, expecting the body to bear it. Since God our

Lord knows our nature infinitely better than we know it, many times, in the course of the changes in penance mentioned, God gives each individual a feel for what suits him.

Note IV. The Particular Examen of Conscience should be made [90] to get rid of failures or carelessness in doing the Exercises and observing the Additions, right through the Second, Third, and Fourth Weeks.

✤ **Comment 9** ✤

# Turning from Sin to Gratitude

You have come to the end of the First Week. In a thirty-day retreat, you are on the ninth or tenth day; in Exercises at home, around the end of the third month.

On rare occasions, people need more time to absorb the First Week, so that your director may add meditations on death and judgment. Also rarely, a man or woman will not honestly accept the gifts of repentance and metanoia. One person refused to acknowledge as sinful a relationship that violated several moral standards. Another kept going over unhappy past events, miserably unwilling to let go of resentment. Another would not believe God tender and loving because God had endowed him with a homosexual orientation. Ignatius did not give up on such persons, whom he described in Annotation 18. He sometimes judged that they would get good out of some meditations on Jesus' life, but he would not take them through the Exercises on making elections and choices. Hence, at this juncture, their directors would understand their change of agenda and give every help for them to accept themselves and the way things actually are.

If you have accepted the gifts of the prayer, you have set aside everything false and all pretending. You have felt the horror of a dynamic that eats you up and destroys you, a dynamic that you have willingly lent yourself to. You have accepted the interior knowledge that this force is still at work in yourself, and that you are powerless but not helpless before it. You know in whose Name your help lies.

This graced knowledge does not leave you depressed, with a negative self-image. On the contrary: You know better than ever how valuable and precious you are to God. Ordinarily, the First Week does indeed end in "a cry of wonder" with a flood of emotion [60], though extroverts and introverts cry differently and God deals with each as God chooses.

This prayer, however, lies far beyond naive optimism. Those who enter into the Exercises more wholeheartedly and openly experience the disorder of sin and sinfulness as a chaos to be called out of, an intractable and insane mess out of which God keeps creating your true self. You have recognized how specific distorted desires have led you to grief and unhappiness and you have begun to experience clearer desires that you somehow know lead to peace. The gratitude that God "has always until now shown me such kindness and mercy" makes you yearn to do something, or hanker for something to do [71]. You have a great sense of owing much to God in Christ.

For the gifts of the First Week do indeed take root in a stronger sense of how sin wrecks humankind and do grow into an abiding sorrow over your own contribution. But they have come to full fruit when you feel a freeing gratitude to God and find joy in the liberating hope that you can discover what it is He wishes in you and through you.

# Second Week

═══ ✚ ═══

✚  **Comment 10**  ✚

# Turning to the Reign of God

After you have finished the First Week in a thirty-day retreat, you spend a kind of transition day. Instead of praying five hours, you will pray an hour in the morning and another later in the day on a meditation called "The Call of the King," or sometimes "The Kingdom." If you are making the Exercises at home, you will simply spend a week praying daily on this material.

The change of rhythm brings you some rest, of course, but you mark important shifts with this day and its contemplation. First, you no longer stand under the cross of the defeated Jesus of Nazareth; you walk with Jesus as He brings Good News to towns and villages. Further, you break out beyond the close, dark horizon of humanity's work of sin and onto the vast horizon of God's work to establish His Reign in the whole world. Your self-appreciation moves subtly from a sinner passively saved to a sinful person invited, amazingly, to labor beside the King in His great enterprise. These shifts do not come as surprises but grow out of your changing relationship with God. And the shifts all take place within your own concrete agenda: You do not escape your sin but by God's gift transcend it, and your own particular gifts will all your life frame the call of the One who gives them to you.

Your director may well ask you at this point whether you desire to go on. Ignatius would not continue an exercitant into the next three Weeks unless the exercitant had a great desire to go into them. That desire — to continue in the Spiritual Exercises a search for something more — itself comes as a gift from the Spirit of God.

## The Contemplation on the Kingdom

Scholars and directors consider this contemplation very important. They consider it Ignatius's creation, though he had almost surely pondered something like it in a preface to the *Lives of the Saints* that he had read and reread on his sickbed. During the first months of his penitential life, Ignatius had found great good in considering Jesus Christ as a king, and had come to a way of praying in this matter that gave him courage and lifted his vision.

Doubtless working out of his own experiences, Ignatius gave his meditation a two-part format, first a fantasy of a great human king and then a meditation on Jesus Christ as king.

You imagine, first, a great king who proposes to labor and suffer and risk in order to conquer the world. In Ignatius's day, men and women going through the Exercises would be immediately stirred by such a splendid leader and such a great enterprise as "conquering all the domains of the infidels." Recall that the year Iñigo was born, Europeans began colonizing the Western Hemisphere, beginning the emergence of global humanity. By the time Iñigo reached boyhood, Vasco da Gama had reported to Europe the teeming subcontinent of India. The year before Iñigo was wounded, Portuguese traders opened a door into China, and a year later, Hernando Cortes dismantled the Aztec state and imposed Spanish control on Mexico.

The new horizons kept opening. During the years when Ignatius and his Companions were giving the Exercises, the Portuguese colonized Brazil and reached Japan, and the French sailed up the St. Lawrence River. Just as Ignatius finished writing his last draft of the *Spiritual Exercises*, Coronado went up into New Mexico and Texas.

Europe tingled with the excitement of these far realms filled with gold and other wealth (chocolate, lumber, pelts), but also filled with people who had never heard of Jesus Christ. Imaginations were inflamed by reports from Franciscans, Dominicans, and *beatas*, single women who went to the infidel to teach religion. One horizon after another rose for spiritual conquest.

## The Call of Christ the King

Now Ignatius asks the one going through the Exercises to turn to Jesus Christ. The parable about a great king summoning his subjects to go and conquer all the infidel lands had prepared the people whom Ignatius directed to cast the call of Christ onto a much larger horizon than they had been living within. In point of historical fact, scores and then hundreds of young men were drawn over these new horizons into the missions. One famous instance: Fired by thoughts of Christ the King, Francis Xavier was in India by 1542, and when Ignatius died in 1556, seventy-eight others had been fired by these same thoughts and had joined his mission there.

Directors today have discovered that they have to adjust this parable for most people going through the Exercises. They find few people, in this age of revolution and democracy, stirred by a king, even a visionary king. Further, we do not make so drastic a distinction between the fate of those within and those outside of the Christian communion. Yet all of us can be moved strongly by great leaders, and your director will almost surely try to find some parable that will open your spirit to the sweeping summons you are about to hear from Jesus Christ. You might consider a great political leader in an emerging country or a great statesman leading the United Nations. One Irish woman used a mythic figure from her nation's history, and an African man used a heroic leader of his tribe.

Whatever you do with the fantasy, you need to note that it is not an analogy: You will not reason from the call of the king to the call of Jesus Christ. You deal here rather with images, dreams, and affects. You want to feel the excitement of a call to transcend everyday concerns. You want to feel the thrill in the story of a great leader doing great things. When you feel that excitement and thrill, then you turn to a real leader and a real project. Now think: You are called to labor, to suffer, and to overcome with this Leader. Now decide: What is your response?

## Two Ways to Respond

We need to recall here that even the desire to follow Jesus Christ faithfully comes to you as a gift from God's Spirit. So when we talk presently about a self-offering, we are not talking about something you initiate. Rather, you discover an invitation rising within yourself to follow Jesus Christ and perhaps to imitate Him. No one can create an authentic desire of this kind in the self, though its seeds are planted in us at baptism; but each of us must, with God, create our own response.

Ignatius suggests two possible responses. One is the response of anyone with sense: To join willingly in this great enterprise as a cooperator. Practically, this means to say yes to redemption in Christ Jesus and to live a life according to the Commandments. One of the fine effects of the Spiritual Exercises is to come to know that your ordinary Christian life contributes to a divine enterprise.

The second response is to hope to go beyond that and to join those who make what Ignatius calls "an offering of greater worth and moment." Of greater worth, because they offer themselves and not just their work; of greater moment, because the Spirit can then raise in them effective desires that shape others' destinies. For these generous women and men, Ignatius writes a prayer of self-offering (he does this in only one other Exercise, "Contemplation to Reach Love").

Is such an offering an idealistic dream? Can it ever really happen? History suggests the answer: It happened when hundreds and hundreds of men chose to live self-sacrificing lives dedicated to instructing the young, making Jesuits the schoolmasters of Europe. It still happens as religious women leave good positions and go live on the land among the poor in Appalachia. It happens when women and men leave a secure life of plenty and go work abroad among oppressed peons in daily danger of being murdered. It still happens.

This fuller response does not rise from dedication to an ideal. It rises from a personal love for Jesus Christ that wishes somehow to do more, to be more intimately engaged with the Lord in this labor, to be a closer follower. From now on, you will beg God for a specific gift: to know Jesus better, to love Him more, and to follow Him, wherever He will lead you.

## ✤ Ignatian Text ✤

# The Call of the King [91]

*The call of an earthly king helps us contemplate the life of the Eternal King.*

Readiness Prayer. The Readiness Prayer will be the usual one.

First Prelude. I compose myself by imagining the place. Here I imagine myself gazing on the synagogues, villages, and towns where Christ our Lord used to go preaching.

Second Prelude. The second Prelude is to beg the grace I want. Here I will ask from our Lord the grace not to be deaf to His call, but quick and diligent to fulfill His most holy will.

**First Part** [92]

First Point. The first point is to see with my mind's eye a human king who has been chosen by God our Lord Himself and to whom all leaders and all Christian peoples show reverence and give obedience.

Second Point. The second point is to observe how this king ad- [93] dresses all his people, telling them, "It is my will to conquer all the domains of the infidels. And so, if anyone wants to accompany me, he will have to be content to eat as I eat, and to drink, and to dress, and all the rest. And at the same time, he will have to work with me during the day and watch with me during the night, and so on. For this way, having shared with me in the labor, he will share with me in the victory."

Third Point. Thirdly, I consider what response good subjects [94] should give to so open and noble a king; and consequently, how anyone who should reject the invitation of such a king would deserve to be reviled by absolutely everybody and to be looked on as a depraved knight.

## [95] Second Part

*The second part of this Exercise is done by applying to Christ our Lord the example of the earthly king just given, following the three points that were mentioned.*

First Point. Taking up the first point: If a call such as this from an earthly king deserves attention, how much more worthy of consideration is it to see Christ our Lord, the eternal King, with all the peoples of the whole world attending to Him. To all together and to each one individually, He gives this call: "My will is to conquer the whole world and all enemies, and so to enter into the glory of My Father. Whoever, then, wishes to accompany me must share the labor with me, so that following me in the suffering, he may also follow me in the glory."

[96]     Second Point. The second point is to ponder that all those who have a sound mind and good judgment will offer themselves entirely for this work.

[97]     Third Point. There are those who feel greater desires to show devotion to their eternal King and universal Lord, and to distinguish themselves by serving Him completely. They will not only offer themselves for this work, but also, going against their sensuality and against carnal and earthly love, they will make offerings of greater worth and moment, saying:

[98]     Eternal Lord of all things, in the presence of your infinite Goodness and before your glorious mother and all the saints of the heavenly court, with your grace and help, I make this offering. I want and desire, and it is my deliberate determination — provided only that it would be to your greater service and praise — to imitate You in bearing all injuries, all reproaches, and all poverty, actual as well as spiritual, if your Divine Majesty will choose me for such a way and state of life and receive me into it.

[99]     Note I. This Exercise should be made twice during the day, that is to say, in the morning on getting up and one hour before the noon or the evening meal.

[100]     Note II. During the Second Week, and from then on, it is very profitable to spend some brief periods reading from the book of *The Imitation of Christ*, or from the Gospels, or in the lives of the saints.

## ❖ Comment 11 ❖

# The Prayer of the Second Week

Ignatius assigns twelve days' material for the Second Week. Directors today regularly keep you at least ten days in this Week, and one standard form of the Exercises at home keeps you for fourteen weeks. You use this material to pray through the saving events in the life of Jesus of Nazareth, starting with His conception and ending (in this Week) with His entry into Jerusalem on a donkey. Each day of this week, you will turn to two events in Jesus' life, or perhaps a single one, and pray on that five times.

During the first three days, you contemplate the Incarnation and the infancy of Jesus of Nazareth. On the fourth, you go through some special Ignatian Exercises. Then during the remaining days, perhaps six or eight, you follow Jesus in His public life and ministry.

You ask the Spirit to guide you through two tightly interrelated developments during these days: to grow personally closer to Jesus Christ, and to grow clearer about and readier for the important options in your life.

### The Intimate Knowledge of Jesus

Ignatius lived at a time when the imitation of Christ had long been established as a leitmotif of the spiritual life. He found the tradition well developed in the pages of the books he read and reread during his convalescence and explicitly embodied in the pages of *The Imitation of Christ*. The tradition taught him to imitate Jesus of Nazareth, "born in extreme poverty so that . . . He can die on the cross" [116].

As these days go by one after another, you do not remain on the surface of events in Jesus' life but go well past externals. You ask the Lord to let you feel what He felt when, for instance, He saw the widow of Naim following the body of her only son. You ask to follow His thinking when He explained to a scribe the Greatest

Commandment. You want to be delighted with His delight when the children climb all over Him.

You enter into the history of Jesus' redemptive act, the "salvation story" and its "saving events," as that history is called here. You do not just remember; you *enter into* the events. How this can happen is a mystery; but Jesuit theologian Karl Rahner reminds us that while we must go through one event after another and our history stretches sequentially in time, in God all things are now. As you are contemplating Jesus' birth today in your city, in God Jesus is being born in Bethlehem. Many giants of prayer wrote about Jesus' life as though they had been there: St. Augustine, St. Bernard, Ludolph the Carthusian. As you enter more deeply into this Week, you will know that in some genuine sense, they had been.

For by God's gift you will be, as well. You do not merely watch Peter fall at Jesus' feet after He had calmed wind and waves; you feel the heave of the boat and even the same unworthiness. You hear Jesus speaking to you. You feel the goodness of His mother's concern at Cana and the amazement of the guests. You know the glee Zacchaeus felt, and the Master's joy at the little man's generous response. In these experiences, you are coming to be a follower of Jesus Christ, who is becoming your way.

You learn this about yourself, actually, because intimate knowledge cuts two ways: As you come to know another intimately, you come to know yourself more deeply. As you enter with great reverence into the heart and mind of the Savior, you enter more deeply into your own heart, discovering with similar reverence what He has already put there and wants now to put there.

This dual intimacy informs your constant reflection upon yourself. You are learning who you are, in Christ, and as you walk with Him, through each event of His life, you know more and more clearly what you most authentically want. Notions that seemed idealistic pipedreams — of a dedicated life, of a genuine Christian marriage, of a single professional life in service — begin to feel like what you have come into the world to do. The career you took up almost for lack of anything better to do takes on the aspect of an adventure with Christ. Your present duties that have been nothing but burdens transmute into a share in Jesus' care for His own.

## Contemplative in Action

In these days, then, you contemplate the life of Jesus Christ for a specific purpose. As the church has from the very beginning, you ask over and over in your third Prelude to know Jesus Christ, to love Jesus Christ, and to follow Jesus Christ. Many who have received this grace have lived it out in a cloistered life of contemplation and communion with Christ. The desire to know Jesus Christ that you are growing into differs somewhat (though it has more than once moved a man or woman into a cloistered life of contemplation). You are asking for a communion in Jesus Christ's concrete hopes and desires.

What does He want for humankind, for the church, and for your life world? How can you share in His desiring? You are seeking "communion" in its root sense here: The Latin *cum* means together with, and *munus* means obligatory services or duty. "Communion" with Christ, then, means being united with Him as He does what God's will requires of Him. You seek communion with God acting in the world, continuing busily to create and govern, continuing to bring the Reign. You and you alone can know what the *munus* is that Christ summons you to, and you can know it only in dialogue with Him. This is why you want and beg to know and love Jesus Christ here — because then you will know how you are to follow Him.

Not surprisingly, the Spiritual Exercises most characteristically produce, not the quiet contemplative in retirement, but what one of Ignatius's friends called the "contemplative in action": contemplative, because always seeking God making the world and always listening to God's hopes rise in your own desires; in action, because always acting in imitation of the Master in action.

## Continuing in Contemplation

Besides examining your life, self, and actions, you have spent time during the past days fantasizing, meditating, and beginning to contemplate. During this Week, you will find yourself invited to learn another way to pray mentally, called "the application of the senses."

The application of the senses had a long history in Catholic spiritual writing before Ignatius. It belongs to that kind of prayer called "kataphatic," meaning filled with images and words. It is a completely incarnated prayer, remaining wrapped in senses. Ignatius could have found instruction in the method from Benedictines at Montserrat, the Dominicans in Manresa, or the Carthusians he and his friends visited every Sunday in the suburbs of Paris. Ignatius directs the exercitant to use this method in the fifth hour of the day, plainly because it is simple, quiet, and more affective than discursive.

People actually use this method of the senses all the time. When your go back over an event in your mind, say an automobile crash, you remember it by taking one thing at a time. You might recall first who did what and when: which car came which way, how they collided. Then you might note what was said, by whom, and to whom: who shouted, accused, wept, apologized. You will remember details of smell like the sharp odor of battery acid and of color like the ruby blood on a face. And in all this, you are resting in the whole feel of the event, in its tensions and so forth. You are applying your senses to this event.

You will do the same to a saving event in Jesus' life, say to the healing of the Gerasene demoniac, after you have meditated on it and contemplated through it several times. You sit still, as though remembering. You seem to hear Jesus' voice and the squeal of the swine leaping into the sea as though you had heard them before. You may well spend a full hour simply savoring, with a kind of spiritual purr, the touch of Jesus' hand on the demoniac's bruised face.

You might note something here about praying with Scripture. Christians of Ignatius's day accepted the words of Scripture as verbatim reports of events and did not doubt that Jesus had said exactly what the Latin Gospels report. We are not likely to think the same, but we readily enter into the salvation story and as we come to know Jesus of Nazareth, hermeneutical problems fall into perspective. Some novices have a problem praying with the Scriptures, often enough because of recently learned theories of interpretation. But even the learned may have trouble; one theologian trained in hermeneutics was never sure that he contemplated real events until in one of his contemplations he touched the wood of the cross. Then he knew. Should you find problems with some saving event, say, contemplating the slaughter of the innocents or the multiplication of the loaves, your director will likely suggest that you omit it.

### The Contemplations on the Infancy

You begin the prayer of this Week at midnight, fantasizing how the triune God might encompass the whole earth and determine to redeem humankind from its death-dealing. You then contemplate the Nativity as the day dawns, bringing Jesus Christ into the world.

This begins the major work of the Second Week: attending in faith and hope to the grand project of God, ongoing creation and ongoing redemption, into which you have been summoned and invited. Your contemplation will raise questions about personal commitment to this project: Can you accept that humankind make up God's hopes for the earth, and perhaps for much more? At what level does Jesus summon your commitment: Commandments or counsels (the vows of poverty, chastity, and obedience in a religious congregation)? Ordinary life or extraordinary service? The conventional and very good or the principled and more fruitful? Whatever your particular call, if you keep going through these Exercises, you will find a way that, for you in your concrete circumstances, means finding *more*.

## ✤ Ignatian Text ✤

# Incarnation and the Infancy of Jesus

**First Day**                                                            [101]

**First Contemplation**

This is a contemplation of the Incarnation. It includes the Readiness Prayer, three Preludes and three points, and a Colloquy.

Readiness Prayer. The Readiness Prayer will be the same.

[102]     First Prelude. The first Prelude is to recall the salvation story in what I am about to contemplate. Here I recall how the Three Divine Persons gazed upon the vast sweep of the earth, around the whole globe, fully peopled. I recall how, watching the multitude sinking down into Hell, They make the decision deep in eternity that the Second Person should become human in order to save the human race. And so, when the fullness of time came, the Divine Persons sent the holy angel Gabriel to Our Lady. See Luke 1:26–38.

[103]     Second Prelude. The second Prelude is to compose myself in the place. Here I envision the full sweep and circle of the earth, where there are so many and such different peoples. And then, coming down to the particular, in the province of Galilee, in the town of Nazareth, I see the house and the chamber of Our Lady.

[104]     Third Prelude. The third Prelude is to ask for what I want. Now I beg for an intimate knowledge of the Lord who has made Himself human for me, so that I might better love Him and follow Him.

[105]     Note. Here is a good place to note that this same Readiness Prayer — done without change, as was said at the beginning — and these three Preludes are to be made during this Week and in the Weeks that follow. The Preludes take shape from the changing subject matters.

[106]     First Point. The first point is to see the persons on either side.

So, first: I see the peoples of earth in all their diversity of costume and mores. Some are light-skinned and some are dark-skinned; some at peace and others warring; some weeping and others laughing; some healthy and others sick; some are being born and others are dying; and so on.

Second: I see and ponder over the Three Divine Persons on their royal dais or seated on the throne of Divine Majesty. They gaze upon the full sweep and circle of the earth and see how all the peoples, living in such blindness, die and go down into Hell.

Third: I watch Our Lady and the angel who is greeting her.

Then I do some reflecting to find profit from this whole scene.

[107]     Second Point. The second point is to listen to what individuals are saying all around this world, that is, how they talk with each other, how they swear and blaspheme, and so on. Likewise, I hear what the three Divine Persons are saying, which is, "Let us work out the redemption of the human race," and so on. Then, what the angel and Our Lady say.

And after that, I do some reflecting to find profit in what they say.

Third Point. The third point is to watch what the people all [108] around the world are doing, that is, wounding, killing, going down to Hell. Likewise, what the Divine Persons are doing, that is, working out the most holy Incarnation and the rest. And in the same way, what the angel and Our Lady are doing, that is, the angel carrying out his office of ambassador and Our Lady humbling herself and giving thanks to the Divine Majesty.

And after that, I do some reflecting to find what is profitable in each one of these things.

At the end a Colloquy is to be made. I think over what I ought to [109] say to the Three Divine Persons, or to the eternal Word Incarnate, or to His mother, Our Lady. I will shape petitions out of what I have felt, leading to a closer following and imitation of our Lord now newly incarnate.

I close with the Our Father.

## Second Contemplation [110]

*The second contemplation is of the Nativity.*

Readiness Prayer. The Readiness Prayer will be the same.

First Prelude. The first Prelude is the salvation story, which this [111] time is how Our Lady, pregnant now for about nine months and (as may piously be believed) seated on a donkey, set out from Nazareth. With her went Joseph and a serving maid who was leading an ox. They travel toward Bethlehem to pay the tribute imposed by Caesar on all those lands (see Luke 2:1–14).

Second Prelude. The second Prelude is to compose myself in [112] the place. Here it will be seeing with the eye of the imagination the road from Nazareth to Bethlehem, considering how long it is and how wide, and whether it is level or goes through valleys and over hills. In the same way, it will be seeing the place or the cave of the Nativity, considering whether it is large or small, deep or high, and how it is arranged.

Third Prelude. The third Prelude will be the same as in the [113] preceding contemplation and in the same form.

First Point. The first point is to see the persons, that is to say, [114] to see Our Lady and Joseph and the serving maid and, after He is born, the infant Jesus. I turn myself into a poor and unworthy little servant, watching them, contemplating them, serving them in their needs as though I were actually there, utterly tactful and reverent. And after that, I reflect on myself so as to find some profit.

[115]     Second Point. The second point is to attend to, carefully consider, and contemplate what these persons are saying, and then reflect on myself so as to find some profit.

[116]     Third Point. The third point is to watch and ponder what they are doing, for instance, in the case of the journeying and the laboring, how they are done so that the Lord can be born in extreme poverty, so that, at the end of tremendous struggles with hunger and thirst, heat and cold, injuries and affronts, He can die on the cross. And all this for me. And after that, I do some reflecting to find some spiritual profit.

[117]     Colloquy. Close with a Colloquy, the same as in the preceding contemplation, and with an Our Father.

### [118] Third Contemplation

*The third contemplation is a repetition of the first and second Exercises.*

After the Readiness Prayer and the three Preludes, the exercitant makes a repetition of the first and second Exercises. In doing this, he always attends to those more important points where he felt some illumination, consolation, or desolation. And as before, close with a Colloquy at the end and with an Our Father.

[119]     Note. In this repetition and in all those to come, the same order of proceeding should be kept as was kept in the repetitions during the First Week, changing the subject matter of the prayer but keeping the same format.

### [120] Fourth Contemplation

*The fourth contemplation will be a repetition of the first and second, made in the same way as the repetition given just above.*

### [121] Fifth Contemplation

*The fifth contemplation will be to apply the five senses to the first and second contemplations.*

Readiness Prayer. After the Readiness Prayer and the three Preludes, it will be fruitful, using the imagination, to bring the five senses to bear on the first and second contemplations, in the following way.

First Point. The first point is to see the persons with the eye [122] of the imagination, meditating and contemplating in detail their situation and surroundings, and gathering some fruit from the sight.

Second Point. The second point is to imagine hearing what they [123] say, or what they might say, and reflecting on myself to gather some fruit.

Third Point. The third point is to imagine I smell and taste the [124] infinite savor and sweetness of the Divinity, then of the soul, and then of its virtues — and of whatever else can be sensed about the person contemplated. Then reflecting on myself, I gather the fruit of this.

Fourth Point. The fourth point is to imagine touching, for ex- [125] ample, by embracing and kissing the place where the persons step or sit, always being careful to derive some fruit from this.

Colloquy. Close with a Colloquy, as in the first and second [126] contemplations, and with the Our Father.

### Notes

Note I. This is to be noted concerning this Week and the Weeks [127] that follow: I am to read only the saving event that I am presently to contemplate. Consequently, for the time being, I would not read any saving event that I am not going to contemplate on the current day or in the coming hour. This is in order to keep the consideration of one saving event from hampering the consideration of another.

Note II. The first Exercise on the Incarnation is to be made at [128] midnight; the second, at daybreak; the third, at the time of Mass; the fourth, at the hour of Vespers; the fifth, before the time of the evening meal. Each of these five Exercises is to continue for an hour. This same order should be kept on all the following days.

Note III. This is to be observed about a person who is old or [129] weak, or even about a strong person who comes out of the First Week in any way weakened: During the Second Week, it is better that he not rise at midnight, at least some of the time. He ought to make one contemplation in the morning, another at the time of Mass, another before the noonday meal, and then a repetition of these at the time of Vespers, and finally an application of the senses before the evening meal.

[130]     Note IV. Of the ten Additions mentioned in the First Week, the following need to be changed for the Second Week: the second, sixth, seventh, and a part of the tenth.

In the second, the change will be to fix my attention as soon as I wake up on the contemplation that I am to make, wanting to know the eternal Word Incarnate more intimately so that I can serve and follow Him better.

And the sixth will be to call to mind frequently the saving events and the life experience of Christ our Lord, starting with the Incarnation and coming up to the passage or saving event that I am contemplating.

The seventh will be that he carefully use full light or shuttered light, fine weather or inclement weather, insofar as he might sense that it could be profitable and useful for finding what one making the Exercises desires.

Concerning the tenth Addition, the exercitant will have to conduct himself according to the saving events he is contemplating. Some of them call for penances and others do not.

So in this way, all ten of the Additions are to be followed with considerable care.

[131]     Note V. In all of the Exercises except those at midnight and in the early morning, the equivalent of the second Addition should be followed, in some way such as this: As soon as I become aware that the time has come for an Exercise I am to make, as I proceed to it, I will call to mind where I am going and before Whom, and briefly preview the Exercise. And then, having observed the third Addition, I shall enter into the Exercise.

## [132] Second Day

On the second day, take for the first and the second contemplations the Presentation in the Temple and the Flight into Exile in Egypt. See Luke 2:22–39 and Matthew 2:13–18. On these two contemplations, two repetitions are to be made and then the application of the senses, just the way this was done the day before.

Note. In some cases, even when the one making the Exercises [133]
has an open spirit and strong health, it proves useful to make some
changes starting on this second day and going through the fourth
day, so that he can more readily find what he desires. One contemplation would be at daybreak and the other at the time of Mass.
Then, the repetition of the two would be at the time of Vespers,
and the application of the senses before the evening meal.

### Third Day                                                      [134]

On the third day: how the child Jesus was obedient to his parents
in Nazareth. See Luke 2:51–52. Then how they later found Him
in the Temple. See Luke 2:41–50. And following this, do the two
repetitions and the application of the senses.

## ❖ Comment 12 ❖

# Following and Imitating Christ

After the "warmth, and song, and sweetness" of prayer on Jesus'
Incarnation and infancy, you begin to wonder what more is there?
On the fourth day of the Week, some Ignatian meditations help
you address that question.

In Ignatius's day, the same question was being asked not only
by monks and nuns, but by women and men in everyday life,
part of the tide-change during Ignatius's life. For an earlier tide
had ebbed: At the end of the sixth century, Gregory the Great
had translated the spirituality of Augustine and Cassian into pas-
toral terms and made it available to the clergy and people of the
West. Five hundred years later, at the end of the eleventh century, that had passed and several forms of monasticism (for men
and women both) had drawn all high spirituality into the cloister.
Consequently, during the Middle Ages, Christians tended to distinguish between the ordinary life of keeping the Commandments

and the life of perfection, which generally meant taking the vows of religion in a monastery and leading the life of contemplation.

Ignatius makes the medieval distinction between ordinary and perfect life [135], and retains the church's tradition of thinking highly of the latter. However, he implies throughout the *Spiritual Exercises* that every baptized Christian — in the marketplace, in the family, in the cloister — is liable to hear the call to the most complete following and imitation of Christ.

In this particular, Ignatius's spirituality suits the twentieth century well. With the Second Vatican Council, we have embraced the priesthood of the laity and expect that every mature Christian will have a spirituality. The Spiritual Exercises proceed on the assumption that every baptized person is a disciple of Jesus and that among us are those called to imitate Jesus in an evangelical life in poverty or in some selfless service in marketplace or church. The Ignatian Exercises on this fourth day hope to open you further to the possibility that you have such a call from God your Creator and Lord.

### The Two Standards

This meditation is Ignatius's invention. He is applying to everyday life the belief, expounded vividly in the Gospel of John, that human existence is a struggle between light and dark, life and death, truth and the lie. He learned in the *Life of the Saints* how St. Augustine opposed the City of God to the city of fallen humankind and found there a description of Jesus as King in Jerusalem opposed by Satan, who reigned in Babylon.

In this meditation, you fantasize the ugly seat of the Liar and the lovely throne of the true Leader, Jesus. You meditate on two opposed strategies. The strategy of the Evil One starts in the way things are with wealth. Money means privilege and power, and the privileged and powerful find ways to get money. The monied buy the best health care and legal advice. They are given attention when they demand it. They grow famous, acquire authority, and their tastes and opinions are honored whether they have inner worth or not.

This is the way things are, and the Opponent uses it. His strategy for you: First you learn to dote on the things you have. Then you notice that you are the one with these things. Then you grow convinced that you have a right to these things and to any others you come to yearn for. So far, you will have committed no sin. But once you have adopted the belief that you have a right to all that you have, you have elected to decide for yourself what will make you happy. Eventually, you will try to choose even your original purpose. This is pride, which makes you liable to a serious fall from grace.

Jesus chose a different strategy and invites you to follow Him. He knows how wealth works and also how you learn to live humbly. His strategy for you: First recall that everything you have is a gift, always being given you. Then, realize that you do not depend on any creature but only on the Creator of all and may therefore choose to have little of anything. Then you ask God to give you little of anything, particularly of fame and worldly success, if God wills to grant you that as He did to Jesus.

Whether or not God grants you to desire to imitate Jesus, you follow His strategy in its root by determining to live fundamentally grateful. That you can never relinquish. But you may not be able honestly to ask God to grant you poverty or the desire to live poor. You may not have the gift to make this prayer, a gift that God does not give to every Christian, by any means. You may not even want to desire it. You may not even be able to imagine what possible good could come from poverty and hiddenness.

Should you wish you could imitate Jesus, or should you judge that you are offered the gift to live in evangelical poverty and are resisting it deep in yourself, you might pray for the gift of desiring poverty and hiddenness [157]. Keep in mind that God communicates the divine hopes in us precisely within our authentic desiring.

## Three Sorts of People

In these original Exercises, Ignatius is drawing you back through many of the considerations of the Principle and Foundation, now at another level, preparing you more immediately as you move to some election, choice, or decisions. In this Exercise, he reminds you again of active indifference.

He divides all those who want to serve God into three sorts. You needn't think of sociological cohorts here; rather, think of people following certain patterns in their lives, of whom you might say, "They are just that sort of people." Ignatius is picking up a usage of moral theologians, who commonly presented moral situations by talking about pairs or couples of people (one manuscript calls this Exercise "Three Pairs of People").

Postulate that these men and women lead good, spiritual lives. They have honestly acquired considerable wealth. Inexplicably, that leaves them spiritually uneasy, though they do not know why. Being spiritually sensitive, they want to shake off that uneasiness.

The first sort of people are those who would do nothing. The second sort, intending to keep the wealth, would do something to assuage their uneasiness in order to be able to keep the wealth in peace. The third sort do nothing at all until they can decide what God wants of them, for they are equally willing to keep the wealth or to let go of it. They look first and in everything to find what God hopes in them and stand indifferent to wealth or poverty, long life, or short, and so on.

Men and women today do not often find great fervor in this consideration, but it can challenge you to renew the grace of the Principle and Foundation, the grace of active indifference.

### Three Models of Following Christ

On the fifth day of the Second Week, you watch Jesus tell His mother goodbye and follow Him from Nazareth to Jordan, where He is baptized. For the next six or eight days, you will contemplate Jesus as He goes about His public life.

During these days, Ignatius urges that you keep in mind three ways to enact your creaturehood and to show your love for God, "Three Models of Humility." A " model" here means a concrete design of operation, like a model of democratic government or different models of friendship and marriage. You do not make a formal hour of prayer on these models, but muse about them between times of prayer.

Humility means first of all a right relationship with God our Creator and Lord and then with your own self, both of which relations you embody and manifest in your relationships with others. You are humble when you recognize your creaturehood in its concreteness, saying yes to all those things in yourself that you did not choose (your sex, for instance, and your intelligence level). You are then able to see your self and your life world as they really are, for as the saints say, humility is truth.

However, this truth is not theoretical; this is the truth that you enact and live out. Humility is a way of doing, not just a way of feeling. Ignatius suggests that you can be called by the Holy Spirit to do this truth in one of three ways.

The first model: You live the first model of humility by keeping the Commandments [165]. You love God to the point of not wanting to be separated from Him. Note that Jesus told the rich young man that this way leads to salvation. Those who keep the Commandments lead a good and holy life.

The second model: You may come to love God more fully and hone your conscience to the point of avoiding any deliberate sins at all [166]. Your truth penetrates more deeply; you see selfishness and avoid it, you look steadily for ways to love better. You need strong active indifference to achieve this and a practiced ability to tame your unruly appetites.

These two models of humility are ways of *following* Jesus the Christ, of living as his disciples and keeping his commands. The third is the way of *imitating* Jesus of Nazareth, of trying to live as obscure and powerless a life as he did [167].

The third model: You accept the gift of loving Jesus and the further gift of having that love at the center of your self. You would like nothing as much as to live as Jesus of Nazareth lived, poor, unknown, and a failure in the eyes of his powerful contemporaries. You would gladly do a great work for the Reign of God, provided that it was hidden or considered unimportant.

Your love for God your Creator and Lord is such, however, that you do not insist that God grant you to live in actual poverty or to undergo actual persecutions as Jesus did, so you wait to see what God the Lord gives to you. Toward suffering and oppression, you might think in one of two ways: You would be willing to accept them were they to come, for Jesus' sake; or you wish that God would indeed visit them on you, for Jesus' sake.

The young Peter Canisius, at the end of this thirty-day retreat, vowed to live without money or resources — except those that his superiors in the Jesuit order instructed him to use. He vowed this because he had come to love Jesus of Nazareth, and to love a leader ordinarily entails wanting to be like him, to imitate him.

The choice laid out starkly by Ignatius's text conveys a perhaps misleading sense of drama. The third kind of humility seems agonistic and full of fury. In real life, it rarely is. Men and women actually elect states in life or choose ways of living that mean a lifelong sacrifice to them but seem to others altogether ordinary. You could be facing such an election or choice, like one of these actual decisions: to live single serving as a parish coordinator; to go to Latin America and labor among the poorest for as long as you can and are allowed; to finish a doctorate and face the testing of university life; to forgo marriage to become a priest; to read, study, and pray daily for the rest of your days for your own sake and your family's.

Intentionally undertaken, many states and styles of life today include embracing hiddenness, risk, deprivation, and the frightening sacrifice of letting solid talents wither or go unused. During the Exercises, you are likely to see some things in your life that offer genuine ways of imitating Jesus of Nazareth. Your insight may also be an invitation.

## ✤ Ignatian Text ✤

[135]

# Introduction to Considering States in Life

The example that Christ our Lord has given us of the first state in life, that of living by the Commandments, we have already pondered: He became obedient to His parents. His example of the second state in life, that of evangelical perfection, we have also already pondered: He remained in the Temple, leaving His foster father and His mother to devote Himself entirely to serving His eternal Father.

Now, while we go on pondering His life, we will start investigating and asking to know in which state or in what kind of life the Divine Majesty wishes us to give Him service.

So perhaps as some introduction to this, we can note in the next Exercise the project of Christ our Lord and, in contrast to it, that of humanity's enemy. We also note how we need to prepare ourselves to come to spiritual maturity in whatever state or kind of life God our Lord gives us to elect.

## Fourth Day [136]

### A Meditation on Two Standards

*This is a meditation on two standards, the one of Christ, our sovereign leader and Lord, and the other of Satan, deadly enemy of our humanity.*

Readiness Prayer. The Readiness Prayer will be the same.

First Prelude. The first Prelude is the salvation story. Here it will [137] be how Christ calls all people and seeks to have them under His standard; and how Satan wants the contrary, all people under his.

Second Prelude. The second Prelude is to compose myself in [138] the place. Here it will be to envision a broad plain taking in all the region around Jerusalem where the supreme commanding general of the good people is Christ our Lord; and then to envision another plain, around Babylon, where the chief of the enemy is Satan.

Third Prelude. The third Prelude is to ask for what I want. Here [139] it will be to beg for an understanding of the machinations of the evil chief and for help to protect myself against them; and further to beg for knowledge of true life, which the sovereign and real leader reveals, and for the grace of imitating Him.

### First Part: The Standard of Satan

First Point. The first point is to imagine the chief of all the [140] enemies sitting out in the vast plain around Babylon on a great throne made of fire and smoke. His appearance inspires horror and terror.

Second Point. Second, consider how he gathers together de- [141] mons without number, and how he scatters some to one city and some to another until he has reached the whole world, missing no single region, no place, no state of life, and no single individual.

Third Point. Third, consider the address he makes to them, [142] goading them on to lay traps and ready trammels. They are to tempt people first to covet riches (as he very commonly does himself) so that they can more easily attain the empty honor of the world, and after that grow swollen with pride. So, the first stage would be wealth; the second stage, honors; and the third stage, pride. By these three stages, he leads to all other vices.

*Second Part: The Standard of Christ*

[143] In the same way, taking the other side, we need to imagine the sovereign and real leader, who is Christ our Lord.

[144] First Point. The first point is to consider how Christ our Lord positions Himself on a broad plain in that region around Jerusalem, taking a place that is lowly, neat, and lovely.

[145] Second Point. Second, consider how the Lord of the whole world chooses quite a number of persons — apostles, disciples, others — and sends them throughout the whole world to spread his holy teaching among people in every state of life and in every social condition.

[146] Third Point. Third, consider the address Christ our Lord makes to all of His servants and friends whom He is sending out in this enterprise. He charges them to try to help all people by drawing them, first, to embrace the most complete spiritual poverty and — if the Divine Majesty would be served by it and should He choose to elect them for it — to embrace as promptly actual poverty. Then they are to draw people to wish for ignominy and contempt, because humility follows from these experiences.

So there are three stages: first, poverty as opposed to wealth; second, ignominy and contempt as opposed to the honor of the world; and third, humility as opposed to pride. And by these three stages they lead to all other virtues.

[147] Colloquy. First Colloquy, with Our Lady. I beg her to win for me from her Son and Lord the grace of being received under His standard, first in the most complete spiritual poverty and then — if the Divine Majesty would be served by it and should He choose to elect me for it and receive me into it — even in actual poverty. Then, second, I beg to suffer ignominy and contempt, the closer to imitate Him, but only if I can suffer these without anyone's sinning and without displeasing the Divine Majesty. This done, I say a Hail Mary.

Second Colloquy. This is to beg the same of the Son, that He obtain it for me from the Father. And I say the Anima Christi.

Third Colloquy. This is to beg the same of the Father, that He grant it to me. And I say the Our Father.

Note. This Exercise is to be made at midnight and again upon [148] rising. Two repetitions are to be made, one around Mass time and another around the time of Vespers. Every hour should end with the three Colloquies, the one with Our Lady, the one with the Son, and the one with the Father. Then the Exercise on the Three Sorts of People, as follows, is to be made around the time of the evening meal.

## Three Sorts of People                                                    [149]

*On this same fourth day, a meditation is to be made on the Three Sorts of People as a help toward embracing what is better.*

Readiness Prayer. The Readiness Prayer will be the same.

First Prelude. The first Prelude is a salvation story about three [150] different sorts of people. A couple of people in each of the three sorts has acquired ten thousand ducats, not precisely or purely out of love for God. Every one of them desires to attain salvation and to find God our Lord in peace, which means ridding themselves of the burden and the obstacle that their attachment to the money they acquired proves to be.

Second Prelude. The second Prelude is to compose myself in [151] place. Here I will envision myself present in front of God our Lord and all of His saints, as a help to be aware of and to want what would be more pleasing to the Divine Goodness.

Third Prelude. The third Prelude is to ask for what I want. [152] At this point, I beg for the grace to elect whatever will be more to the glory of the Divine Majesty and for the salvation of my soul.

The First Sort of People. The couple of people in this first sort [153] would like to rid themselves of the attachment they feel to what they have acquired. They want to find God the Lord in peace and to secure their salvation. And yet, they use no remedies right up to the hour of death.

The Second Sort of People. The couple of this second sort want [154] to get rid of their attachment, but they want to get rid of it in such a way that they will still keep the money. In a way, they want God to come to what they desire. Had they decided on their own to part with the money in order to find God, even that would have left them in better condition.

[155]     The Third Sort of People. The couple in this third sort of people want to rid themselves of the attachment. But they want to rid themselves of the attachment to the thing acquired without developing an attachment to having it or an attachment to not having it. Rather, they want any desire of having and any desire of not having to depend on how God our Lord will move their wills and also on what would seem to them, in this state of mind, as being for the service and praise of the Divine Majesty.

Meanwhile, they adopt the attitude that they have broken every attachment. They firmly set themselves to desire neither that money nor anything else unless the service of God our Lord move them. In this way, a desire to serve God our Lord better is what moves them to take any thing or to leave it.

[156]     Three Colloquies. The same three Colloquies are made here as were made in the preceding contemplation on the Two Standards.

[157]     Note. Notice that when we feel an attachment contrary to actual poverty, or a revulsion against it — when in fact we are not indifferent to being poor or being wealthy — it will go a long way toward overcoming such disordered affectivity to beg God in the Colloquies, going against our fallen nature, to elect us to actual poverty. We insist that we want it, we beg for it, we plead for it, always stipulating that it be to the service and praise of the Divine Goodness.

## [158] Fifth Day

The contemplation of Christ our Lord's parting journey from Nazareth to the river Jordan, and of how He was baptized. See Matthew 3:13–17.

[159]     Note I. This contemplation is to be made once at midnight and again in the morning. Two repetitions of it are to be made, at Mass time and at the time of Vespers, and an application of the five senses before the evening meal. Each of these five Exercises begins with the usual Readiness Prayer and the three Preludes, as all of this has been explained for the contemplation on the Incarnation and the Nativity, and concludes with the Triple Col-

loquy of the Three Sorts of People, or according to the Note that follows it.

Note II. The Particular Examen after the noon and the evening [160] meals will be about faults and lapses in doing the Exercises and observing the Additions during this day. The same should be done on the rest of the days.

**Sixth Day**                                                            [161]

The contemplation of how Christ our Lord went from the river Jordan to the desert, including the temptations there. See Luke 4:1–13; Matthew 4:1–11. The directives given for the fifth day are to be followed.

**Seventh Day**

How St. Andrew and others followed Christ our Lord. See Mark 1:16–20.

**Eighth Day**

The Sermon on the Mount, which is about the eight Beatitudes. See Matthew 5:1–48.

**Ninth Day**

How Christ our Lord appeared to His disciples across the waves of the sea. See Matthew 14:22–33.

**Tenth Day**

How our Lord was preaching in the Temple. See Luke 19:47–48.

**Eleventh Day**

On the raising of Lazarus. See John 11:1–45.

**Twelfth Day**

On Palm Sunday. See Matthew 21:1–11.

## Notes

[162]    Note I. Note first that each person, according to the time he wishes to spend on the contemplations of this Week, or according to the profit he derives from them, can lengthen or shorten the Week. If he wishes to lengthen it, he might take the saving events of the visit of Our Lady to St. Elizabeth, the Shepherds, the Circumcision of the Infant Jesus, the Three Kings, and some others like them. If he wishes to shorten it, he might even omit some of the ones scheduled. The reasoning behind this: The purpose here is to give an introduction to and a method for contemplating so that it can be done better and more searchingly later on.

[163]    Note II. The materials concerning choices in life will be given, to start with, on the same day as the contemplation of the departure from Nazareth for the Jordan and the baptism, which is the fifth day. The materials are explained below.

[164]    Note III. Before anyone starts to deal with choices in life, in order that he may feel real attachment to the true doctrine of Christ our Lord, he would benefit a good deal from attending to and pondering the following three models of humility. He might muse on them from time to time throughout the day and make the Colloquies as they are explained further on.

### Three Models of Humility

[165]    The First Model of Humility. The first model of humility is necessary for salvation, and is this: As far as lies in my power, I so submit and humble myself that I keep the law of God in every particular. This means that — though others promise to make me lord of all creation, or even though my life depended on it — I would not so much as think about breaking any divine or human commandment that binds me under pain of mortal sin.

[166]    The Second Model of Humility. This model is more spiritually mature than the first, and is this: I find myself no more disposed toward or attracted to having wealth than being poor, to seeking honor than being dishonored, to living a long life or a short life, as long as each alternative is equally to God's service and the salvation of my soul. Along with this, I would not enter into deliberation about committing a venial sin, not for the whole of creation and not to escape being put to death.

The Third Model of Humility. This model is the most spiritually [167] mature humility, and is this: Given that I keep practicing the first and second models, and given that the praise and glory of the Divine Majesty would be the same one way or the other, then for the sake of imitating Christ our Lord and of really being more like Him, I choose and elect poverty with Christ poor rather than wealth, contempt with Christ burdened with it rather than the world's honor. And I prefer to be regarded as a worthless fool for Christ, who was first so regarded, than to be held wise and judicious in the world.

Note. Whoever wants to reach this third model of humility will [168] profit a great deal by making the Triple Colloquy given above with the Three Sorts of People. He should beg our Lord to be pleased to elect him into this third model of humility, greater and better than the others, the better to imitate and to serve — if that would be to the Divine Majesty's equal or greater service and praise.

✤  **Comment 13**  ✤

# Elections, Choices, and Decisions

The text of each Week of the *Spiritual Exercises* ends with some kind of Norms or directives. The First Week ended with the Annotations; this Second Week, with some Norms about the election, choice, or decision. Their position at the end of the Week was Ignatius's way of getting his materials in some order; these Norms have to be mastered by a director before the time of the Exercises begins, and some of their contents may be given to an exercitant earlier or later in the Exercises.

Half a century ago, some scholars contended that you made the full, authentic Spiritual Exercises only if you elected a state in life. Ignatius gave no indication that he believed that, though he and his Companions led many to elect a state in life. Ignatius guided the first Companions to make their election of the evangelical life in poverty. Jean Codure, one of them, gave the Exercises to the son of a Viceroy of Naples, who chose to serve God in the family's hereditary titles. Jerónimo Domènech gave them to a number of people in Valencia in 1552, all of whom elected to enter cloistered life.

Ignatius helped others, however, who were already settled in a state in life; in Rome, for instance, Cardinal Gaspare Contarini. Alfonso Salmerón directed an abbot and the same Domènech in the same place gave the Exercises to four married women. Furthermore, Ignatius included a long, explicit paragraph: "For Amending and Reforming the Way and State in Life" [189].

Perhaps a good way to understand what people face in the Exercises is to distinguish (as these comments have been doing) among election, choice, and decision, remembering that Ignatius does not make the distinction consistently.

"Election" to Ignatius generally means determining whether to live single or married, in religion or not, in orders or not. Directors still help women and men make such elections.

"Choices" have to do with serious options concerning life and lifestyle. Some have to ask themselves, for instance, how big a house to have and how much income to spend on themselves [189]. Directors today constantly meet people choosing whether to change careers, how much time they can reasonably give to serve others, and which relationships to cherish or to hedge.

"Decisions," finally, have to do with what you are going to let things mean in your life, or whether you will adopt or hold a certain attitude or take a certain stance — indifference, for instance, or the third model of humility. Some have decided to accept their past with all its weight; some, to resolutely put off a deep-seated resentment. A social worker decided that she was doing the work for others that God wanted her to do, though she had more or less drifted into social work. One civil servant decided to interpret his hardly stimulating work as a way of educating people to put some order in their lives.

The distinction between choices and decisions is not perfect, but people do have the experiences of facing various options on the one hand (they make choices), and on the other, of facing some fairly unalterable reality in their lives that they must deal with (they make decisions). In a certain real sense, decisions are often the concrete matters in which true conversion of heart, or metanoia, takes place.

Some people go through the Exercises to confirm an election or choice they have already made. That's not new; Francis Xavier went through his retreat, led by Ignatius, several months after he had vowed with the Companions to live in poverty and to go to the Holy Land. Most Jesuit novices and many other religious novices elect to enter religion and then make the thirty-day retreat to test and confirm their election.

## A Framework for Elections and Choices

If a director is to help you sort out what options you face and which among them you are prepared at this time to handle, she or he will need a clear frame to think in. Directors find a great deal throughout the book on the topic, but Ignatius summarizes certain matters here.

Ignatius points out, first of all, that some elections and choices are good and some are bad. He is balancing an objective judgment about things good in themselves with the subjective judgment that this particular thing is the good that God hopes for me. The election to marry made by a man and a woman eager to beget and rear children is a good one. The election made by a man and woman to marry when one of them is already well married is a bad one.

Besides good and bad elections and choices, Ignatius suggests about the process that some elections are well made and some are badly made. The woman who prayerfully weighs her cherished independence and her yearning for nuptial union and then elects to marry has elected well. The man who, falling into a lucrative kind of work, chooses to make a lot of money has chosen badly.

Behind these distinctions lies another proper to Ignatius's historical period. As his language indicates, Ignatius considered that some elections and some choices are permanent and cannot or ought not be changed. This is a difficult matter for us. We wonder, Can anyone say "forever"? We tend to feel that a permanent commitment cannot outlast too great a change in the person who made it. Here is one matter in which the Ignatian director will tend to think with the church against our cultural bias.

Directors know, of course, that the church, when reasons are persuasive, declares that the permanent commitment in some ordinations and marriages was not truly made. But the more skilled directors do not consider the Exercises a good vehicle to help someone decide that point. There are other vehicles to help with that decision.

Ignatius suggests an alternative way of handling a good choice badly made, say, a woman married because of a pregnancy or a man took religious vows because all of his friends did. Ignatius suggests an option rather subtler than the blunt alternatives of simply suffering along or renouncing the commitment.

Consistent with his understanding of God's will and God's hopes in us, Ignatius does not see such a commitment as a true call from God. But he does see God as calling us to remain faithful to our permanent commitments, a fidelity that accords with the faithfulness of God. In a given case, you may find it impossible to keep a permanent commitment; no one doubts that this happens honestly, and the church holds no one to the impossible (hence the annulment of marriages, permission for priests to leave and marry, dispensation from religious vows). But Ignatius suggests and experience has shown that people who doubt or fear the reasons why they made a permanent commitment have been able to let God teach them in the Exercises not to doubt or fear, but to live courageously and find joy, and they have reformed their lives.

### The Times of Election

Ignatius found three typical experiences, which he calls "times," of electing a state in life or making a serious choice: first, one that is nearly automatic; second, one arrived at through a lot of emotional and affective upheaval; and third, one worked out in tranquility by simply thinking through the alternatives. Directors find this holds true today.

Why would it be important to note these times? Simply put, the reason is that they help to recognize and to trust elections and choices. A deeply committed person, you may find that you have simply arrived at election and wonder whether you actually have elected. On the other hand, in Ignatius's second time, you may be fiercely torn by emotion to one side of an option and then to another; you may go through such turmoil that you begin to wonder whether God is in this. You need to know that the God of order works in the storm as well in the calm so that you will have the patience to wait for the determination and not try to force it.

And finally, the third time. You may find it altogether strange that an election or choice of singular importance should be made in deep tranquility. One man could hardly believe that he had indeed chosen when he calmly decided to cut off a seriously sinful relationship. You can see how, if you are electing not to marry, you may well worry that you do not feel any great emotion.

God our Lord chooses how His love will move you to determine and you are wise to be content to find yourself in one time or the other. You need also to keep very clearly in mind that neither discernment of spirits nor a method of election results in certitude. They result in hopeful enactment. When you have elected or chosen, therefore, you need to offer your election or choice to God the Lord and beg His acceptance of it [183, 187].

✦ **Ignatian Text** ✦

# An Introduction [169]
# to Determining a Way of Life

In any good election, insofar as it lies within our powers, our aim and intention ought to be very clear. I focus directly on the end for which I am created, which is for the praise of God our Lord and for the salvation of my soul. Then, whatever concrete choices I might make ought to help achieve the end for which I am created.

I must not try to reorder my end and subject it to some means, but always order any means to my end. For example, many people first elect marriage, which is a means, and second to serve God within the marriage, which is their end. Other people do the same thing who first choose to hold an endowed church office and afterward to serve God in it. As is plain, these people do not go directly to God, but expect that God will directly come around to their disordered attachments. They consequently make of the end a means, and of the means an end; and what they ought to seek first of all, they get to only later.

The reasoning again: We have as our first objective to seek to serve God, which is our end, and as secondary objectives to seek an endowed church office or to marry — if that suits me better — which are means to the end.

And so, nothing should move me to make use of those means or to deprive myself of them except this alone, the service and praise of God our Lord and the eternal salvation of my soul.

## [170] Matters for a Choice in Life

*This explores the matters about which choices are to be made. It includes four points and a note.*

First Point. First, it is necessary that all of the options among which we want to choose should be indifferent or good in themselves. And they must be acceptable strategies within our Holy Mother, the hierarchical church, and be neither bad for nor repulsive to her.

[171]     Second Point. Second, some options are classified as unchangeable elections, such as priesthood, marriage, and so forth. Other options are classified as changeable choices; for example, we may accept endowed church offices or resign from them, and we can accept or renounce material goods.

[172]     Third Point. Third, about unchangeable elections: Once the election has been made, there is nothing more to elect because the decision cannot be undone. This is the case with matrimony, priestly ordination, and so forth. If anyone has elected such a life badly, not with due order but under the influence of disordered affections, then his only option is to repent of this and to see to it that he leads a good life in the way he has elected.

Since its determination was indirect and without due order, moreover, such an election does not seem to be a divine vocation. Many people err in this, for they make a prejudiced choice or a bad one and then call it a divine vocation. But every vocation that comes from God is consistently pure, clear, and without admixture of fallen flesh or of any kind of disordered feelings and valuings.

[173]     Fourth Point. Fourth, about changeable choices: If someone has

made a choice in a correct and well-ordered way, without any yielding to fallen flesh or to the world, he has no reason to go back over his choice. Rather, he should perfect himself in his choice as much as he can.

Note. This should be observed about a changeable choice that [174] was not made sincerely and in a well-ordered way. If he desires to bring forth fruit that is noteworthy and very pleasing to God our Lord, then he would profit by going over his choice, now in a correct way.

## Three Times of Election [175]

*There are three times when a healthy and good choice can be made.*

First Time. The first time is when God our Lord moves and draws the free will in such a way that a deeply committed person follows what has been shown to him, not hesitating and not able to hesitate. This is how St. Paul and St. Matthew acted when they followed Christ our Lord.

Second Time. The second time is when someone draws suf- [176] ficient clarity and insight from the experience of consolations and desolations and from the experience of discerning various spirits.

Third Time. The third time is one of calm. Pondering first why [177] any person is born — as we know, to praise God our Lord and to save his soul — and desiring this, a person elects as the means to this end a certain kind of or state in life within the church, so that he may be helped in the service of his Lord and the salvation of his soul.

I called this a time of calm. In it, a person is not roused by one spirit after another. Rather, he uses his natural powers freely and tranquilly.

If a choice in life is not made in the first or the second time, here [178] are two methods for making it in this third time.

## First Method for Making a Healthy and Good Choice

*It includes six points.*

First Point. The first point is to lay out for myself the matter about which I want to make a choice in life. Examples might be some job or an endowed church office to accept or resign from, or anything else that falls under changeable choices.

[179]      Second Point. Second, it is imperative to keep as my objective the end for which I am created, praising God and saving myself. Along with that, I hold myself in indifference, not influenced by any disordered feeling or valuing, which means that I am no more prepared or inclined to take the thing proposed than to leave it, and no more to leave it than to take it. I find myself right in the middle, then, like the pointer on an evenly balanced scale, and ready to follow whatever I might feel to be more to the glory and praise of God our Lord and for the salvation of my own self.

[180]      Third Point. Third, I beg God our Lord to be pleased to move my free will and to put in my spirit what I ought to do about the option proposed, whatever would be more to His praise and glory. I beg to go over things thoroughly and faithfully in my mind and to choose in conformity with His most holy will and good pleasure.

[181]      Fourth Point. Fourth, I reckon up and ponder over the advantages and benefits that would accrue to me if I held the proposed job or endowed church office truly for the praise of God our Lord and my own salvation. And then I ponder the other side, the disadvantages and dangers in holding it.

I do the same thing for the second alternative, not holding the job or office: I contemplate the advantages and benefits of not holding it and then the other side, the disadvantages and dangers.

[182]      Fifth Point. Fifth, after I have worked through and considered every aspect of some concrete option, I watch which alternative my reason favors. This is the way, following the more serious line of reasoning and not some sensual tendency, that I ought to come to a decision about any concrete option.

[183]      Sixth Point. Sixth, having made such a decision, a person ought to take what he has done to prayer before God our Lord, with care and persistence. And he should offer to God the election he has made so that the Divine Majesty may be pleased to accept and to confirm it if it is for His greater service and praise.

## Second Method for Making a Healthy and Good Election [184]

*It includes four guidelines and a note.*

First Guideline. First, the love that moves me and brings me to make a given election ought to come down from on high, from God's love. As a person starts to elect, he feels about himself that his greater or lesser love for what he is settling on comes from his love for his Creator and Lord.

Second Guideline. Second, I imagine a person whom I have [185] never known or seen. Then, as I desire for that person every perfection, I ponder what I would say to him: What might he do and how should he choose for the greater glory of God our Lord and for the greater perfection of his own self? Then I do the same for myself and observe the norm that I proposed to this other.

Third Guideline. Third, as though I were lying on my deathbed, [186] I consider what process and standard I shall then hope to have followed in making my current election. Then, taking them as a norm, I will make my decision completely in conformity with them.

Fourth Guideline. Fourth, wondering and pondering how I [187] will stand on the day of judgment, I think how I shall then wish to have decided in the present matter. And the norm which I will wish then to have observed now, I will indeed observe now, so that I may then find myself full of contentment and joy.

Note. When, for the sake of my eternal salvation and peace, [188] I have followed the guidelines just given, I will make my choice and will offer it to God our Lord according to the sixth point of the First Method of making a choice.

## For Amending and Reforming the Way and State in Life [189]

Something should be noted about people, wealthy or not wealthy, established in a prelacy or in a marriage who have no grounds for changing their permanent election and no great appetite for making choices in matters that they can change.

It is very profitable to give such persons, in place of the election process, a systematic method for amending and reforming the lives that they lead in their particular state. That means setting before each one the original purpose of his creation and of his life and situation: the glory and praise of God our Lord and the salvation of his own self.

If he is to live out this original purpose and attain his end, he will have to ponder and work over — using the Exercises and the methods of making choices outlined above — how large a house he ought to maintain with how large a household, how he might regulate and govern it, and how he ought to teach his people by word and example. He will also have to examine his resources: How much ought he dedicate to house and household? how much to the poor and to other holy works?

And in all this and through all this, he seeks and searches for nothing other than the greater praise and glory of God our Lord.

For everyone should believe that he will make progress in all spiritual concerns just so far as he will have divested himself of his self-love, self-will, and self-interest.

✢  **Comment 14**  ✢

# The Gifts and Graces
# of the Second Week

You have been praying for twenty or twenty-two days and if you are like the vast majority of men and women who go through the Exercises, you are content to have them continue, day by day. Those who make Exercises at home will have a firmly established routine by now, their prayer and deeper everyday issues tightly interwoven. Notice that those who are able to pray little, say twenty minutes a day, may well be finding some peace and happiness but would not find systematic growth and maturing.

What you have experienced in contemplating Jesus' life and finding your authentic desires will of course be utterly singular and personal. Any summary is just suggestive.

You are very likely to have a deepened, or perhaps quite new, relationship with Jesus, a stronger reverence for Him who is Lord, but also a lively sense of what and how He felt and wished. Very probably, you have come to know the people around Jesus and to like one or other of them. As one person exclaimed: "The people are so *alive* — Anna, the Centurion, Peter! I *like* Peter." One of the results of this, you might note in yourself, is a greatly deepened compassion for and patience with others around you.

With that, you have also felt a deep confirmation of your own self, not only acceptable to Jesus but dear to Him. You have experienced meaning in human existence and although you might not say so explicitly you sense your life unfolding out of some deeply secure agenda. You know yourself not only enmeshed in humankind but fellow to every other human person and somehow called to make a difference in others' lives.

In all likelihood, you have found some strong desires in yourself and have a positive sense that what you want most deeply does indeed lead you to God and mark out your way of contributing to the coming of the Reign. You may still be searching for what you truly desire but you are more likely to have made a serious life election such as to marry, or some rather serious choice such as to change careers. Alternatively, you may have come to clarity about some issue that you grasped only vaguely before and have found courage to decide about it, like the man who decided that he would live joyful in spite of certain personality traits that had kept him sorrowing for years.

This gracious process, however, is not automatic. It happens that some have not made an election or a choice; perhaps you have not yet. Or perhaps, as some do, you have elected or chosen but not according to God's hopes or according to your most authentic desires. Both of those are possible.

It is also possible that you have found yourself confronted by Jesus' obedience to the Father and submission to the brokenness of humanity and felt burdened and diminished in belief and hope. One person faced a profound temptation: Why would I want to follow someone all this happened to? What Jesus says remains hard.

If you have elected or chosen, you are grateful for the election or choice that has been given you, even though what you have elected or chosen plainly entails embracing the cross. Here is a great mystery, one that always astounds a director and moves him or her to deeper faith and hope in Christ.

However the days have gone, a person going through the Exercises often enough comes to the last days of the Second Week and begins to taste sorrow. The sorrow may be your own or your life world's, but you may already be entering into the Passion of the Lord.

# Third Week

## ═ ✢ ═

## ✢ Comment 15 ✢

# Contemplating the Lord's Passion

Your director may suggest a fallow afternoon when you have completed the Second Week. If you are like most exercitants, you were not eager to break the flow of your prayer. So at midnight you move to the Last Supper and in the morning to the Agony in the garden at Gethsemane.

You thus begin the round of five hours of prayer a day, contemplating each day two saving events in the Passion, one at midnight and one in the morning. Then you make a repetition of these two, later in the morning and early in the afternoon. Exercitants often find that these repetitions demand self-discipline, first because there is so much matter that it is easier simply to go on than to repeat, but also because it is arduous to return to places either of insight and fervor or of distraction and darkness. In the evening, you make an application of the senses. On the final day of your Week, which Ignatius calls the seventh day, you make less formal prayer, spending the day instead as though it were the Sabbath when Jesus' body lay in the tomb.

By now, you are sure to have left the role of a spectator and to be entering into the event as an actor. You stand among the soldiery or walk into Jerusalem among Jesus' friends. Even as you enter now almost naturally into these events, however, you need to keep reflecting upon yourself.

You have learned that contemplation can be a gentle, sweet activity (one of the reasons why people take readily to centering prayer). In contemplating the Passion, you can be tempted to skate on the emotional surface, moved by the points in each contemplation to weep and sorrow for a time. You will be pulled into the depth of reflection that these sacred events demand and deserve, however, if you keep in mind the three considerations Ignatius adds (as points four, five, and six [195–197]), either considering them separately or folding them into your contemplation.

For you are required by these three considerations — how Jesus suffered in His humanness, how He hid His divine power, how He did this for you — to enter reverently into Jesus' thoughts and feelings, desires and revulsions, as He was betrayed, imprisoned, groundlessly convicted, tortured, and murdered. You will feel His powerlessness; you may be given to share it with Him.

These are terrible events, and you are keeping a death-watch. Of course, you will be tempted to escape. Some people immerse themselves in the welter of detail, distracted by the knots on the whip or the color of the olive trees. Some simply grow inattentive. Some turn Jesus' suffering into a melodrama from which they can distance themselves. We are none of us helped by the historical fact that devotion to the Passion of Christ is at a low ebb, quite the opposite of Ignatius's time and country, where the devotion was vivid and deep. Any of these stratagems would give your director concerns about your election, choice, or decision.

You will seriously pray the Passion only out of love for Jesus of Nazareth. In the First Week you knew Jesus Christ as a sinner knows his or her Savior. In the Second Week, you found yourself, a sinful person, summoned by the Master to be His disciple. In this Week, you hear Jesus call you, no longer servant, but friend. You are still a sinner; but what was a burden of your individual guilt and shame has become, by a kind of divine trick, a load of grief and pain that you are sharing with your Redeemer. One man who had renounced addiction to a sweet sin felt that he should not really be here. He actually felt terror as he began these days. He prayed, and explained simply in his sorrow, "Jesus told me to just stay with Him."

Much of the spiritual work of prayer on Jesus' Passion is just to be with Him. But you have elected or chosen. Particularly if you have elected a way out of the ordinary — true chastity, a life of service, the principled conduct of your business — you know that you are following and imitating Jesus of Nazareth, a grace you have asked for over and over again. Can you stay with Him now? All this is what Jesus chose for you. Are you sure of what you determined for Him?

Even here you are not seeking a personal union with Jesus that will let you lay aside or even escape your own real issues and tasks. One person made that mistake, resolutely setting aside concerns about some hard choices he had made as though they were irrelevant to his sharing in Jesus' sufferings. He found that he was feeling irrelevant, an outsider, and stayed there until he accepted that the hard pieces of interior work he had to handle were, as he said, "where I am now." He laid them at Jesus' feet and then had a strong experience of things being as they are because God wants them as they are. Plainly that experience is related to the earliest prayer in the *Spiritual Exercises*, but it is also central to taking part in the sufferings Jesus "had to undergo."

Directors know that people go through the Third Week in various ways according to many variables of temperament and experience. You may find yourself dry and stiff, like a sponge in a desert; perhaps God is leading you to share Jesus' desperate desolation. Or again, you may find yourself weeping much of the time; your hours may seem like an instant and the days, very short.

One thing is sure: You will not decide how you are going to take part in Jesus' Passion. God's Spirit decides. In this at least, you know His genuine powerlessness.

## ✤ Ignatian Text ✤

[190] # The Passion and Death of Jesus

**First Day**

**First Contemplation**

*This first contemplation is done at midnight. It is a contemplation of how Christ our Lord went from Bethany to Jerusalem and of the Last Supper. See Matthew 26; John 13:1–30. It includes the preparatory prayer, three Preludes, six points, and a Colloquy.*

Readiness Prayer. The Readiness Prayer will be the same.

[191] First Prelude. The first Prelude is to recall the salvation story. This time, it is to remember how Christ our Lord sent two disciples from Bethany to prepare the Supper and then went to it Himself with His other disciples. After they had eaten the Paschal Lamb and finished the Supper, He washed His disciples' feet and gave them His most Holy Body and Precious Blood. And He gave them His discourse after Judas had gone out to sell his Lord.

[192] Second Prelude. The second Prelude is to compose myself in the place. Here I consider the road from Bethany to Jerusalem, seeing whether it is wide or narrow, whether level, and so on. And in the same way I consider the place where the Supper was held, whether it is large or small, arranged in this or that way.

[193] Third Prelude. The third Prelude is to ask for what I want. Now I beg for sorrow, grief, and shame because for my sins the Lord goes to His Passion.

[194] First Point. The first point is to see the persons who are at the Supper. Then I do some reflecting about myself to try to find profit from them.

Second Point. The second point is to listen to what they say and similarly to find profit from it.

Third Point. The third point is to watch what they do and again, to find some profit.

[195] Fourth Point. The fourth point is to ponder over what Christ our Lord suffers humanly, or what He wishes to suffer, within each

of the events that I contemplate. And at this point, I begin to strive with all my might to sorrow, to grieve, and to weep. I labor in the same way through the points that follow.

Fifth Point. The fifth point is to consider how His divinity hides [196] itself; how, that is to say, He can destroy His enemies and does not and how He allows His most holy humanity to suffer most bitterly.

Sixth Point. The sixth point is to consider how He suffers all of [197] this for my sins, and so on. Also to wonder, What ought I do and undergo for Him?

Colloquy. I finish with a Colloquy to Christ our Lord. I close [198] with an Our Father.

Note. Something can be mentioned here that was explained [199] earlier only partly. In a Colloquy, we ought to talk things over and to make petitions according to the subject in the prayer. This means according to whether I find myself tempted or consoled, whether I hope for one virtue or another, want to dispose myself to one option or another, or to rejoice or sorrow over the matter I contemplate. Finally, I beg to have what I more actively long for in some of my special interests.

In doing this, an exercitant might make a single Colloquy with Christ our Lord. Then again, if he is moved by what he contemplates or by his own devotion, he might make three, one with the mother of our Lord, one with her Son, and one with the Father. He would then follow the form given in the meditation on the Three Sorts of People and in the note following that meditation.

## Second Contemplation [200]

*This second contemplation is made in the morning. It will be from the Supper through the events in the Garden. See Matthew 26; Mark 14.*

Readiness Prayer. The Readiness Prayer will be the same.

First Prelude. The first Prelude is the salvation story. This time it [201] is how Christ our Lord came down with His eleven disciples from Mt. Sion, where they had held the Supper, into the Valley of Jehosaphat. He left eight of them behind in the valley and then the other three apart in the Garden. And then as he prayed, He sweat something like drops of blood. And after He had prayed three times to the Father, He awakened the three disciples. And after His enemies had fallen to the ground at the sound of His voice and Judas had given Him the kiss of peace, and after St. Peter had cut off the ear of Malchus and Jesus had put it back in place, they arrested Him as an evildoer. And they led Him down into the valley and up the other side toward the house of Annas.

[202] Second Prelude. The second Prelude is to envision the place. Here I consider the road from Mt. Sion to the Valley of Jehosaphat and also the Garden itself: Is it small? spacious? one kind of landscape or another?

[203] Third Prelude. The third Prelude is to ask for what I want, which here would be what is proper for the Passion: Grief with Christ grieving, heartbreak with Christ heartbroken, weeping, inward pain upon the great pain that Christ suffered for me.

## Notes

[204] First Note. For this second contemplation, after he has made the Readiness Prayer and the three Preludes already given, the exercitant should follow the same manner of proceeding through the points and the Colloquy as he used in the first contemplation on the Supper.

Around the time of Mass and of Vespers, he should make two repetitions of these contemplations — the first and the second — and then before the evening meal, an application of the senses to the two of them. The Readiness Prayer and the three Preludes always come first, adapted to the subject matter and following the way of proceeding given and explained above in the Second Week.

[205] Second Note. Depending on what his age, spiritual condition, and temperament make useful to the one going through the Exercises, he will make five Exercises each day or fewer.

[206] Third Note. During the Third Week, parts of the second and sixth Additions will change.

The second: As soon as I awake I call to mind where I am going and for what purpose, briefly previewing the contemplation I am about to make. In keeping with the saving events, I will make every effort as I rise and dress to sorrow and grieve at the deep sorrow and terrible suffering of Christ our Lord.

The sixth changes this way: I will not let myself entertain joy-filled thoughts, even though they are good and holy ones, for instance, about the Resurrection or about the glory of heaven.

Rather, I will set myself to feel sorrow, suffering, and heartbreak by steadily calling to mind the labors, exhausting toils, and sufferings that Christ our Lord went through from the moment of His birth down to the saving event in His Passion that I currently contemplate.

Fourth Note. The Particular Examen of Conscience is to be [207] made on the Exercises and on the Additions as currently applied, just as was done in the past Week.

## Second Day [208]

At midnight on the second day, the contemplation will be of the events from the Garden to the house of Annas, including events there. See Matthew 26, Luke 22, Mark 14.

In the morning, from the house of Annas to the house of Caiaphas, including events there. See Matthew 26.

Then two repetitions and the application of the senses, as explained above.

## Third Day

At midnight on the third day, from the house of Caiaphas to Pilate's, including events there. See Matthew 27, Luke 23, Mark 15.

In the morning, from Pilate's to Herod's, including events there. See Luke 23.

Then the repetitions and the application of the senses, following the established format.

## Fourth Day

At midnight on the fourth day, from Herod to Pilate, covering only the first half of events in this house. See Matthew 27, Mark 15, Luke 23, John 19.

In the morning, the rest of the events before Pilate. The two repetitions and the application of the senses as explained.

## Fifth Day

At midnight on the fifth day, from the house of Pilate to the nailing to the cross. See John 19:13–22.

In the morning, from His being raised on the cross until Christ died. See John 19:23–37.

Then the repetition and the application of the senses.

## Sixth Day

At midnight on the sixth day, from His being taken down from the cross to reaching the tomb, excluding the burial. See John 19:23–37.

In the morning, from the placing in the tomb to the house where Our Lady stayed after the burial of her Son.

## Seventh Day

At midnight and in the morning of the seventh day, the contemplation is of the whole Passion.

In place of the repetition and the application of the senses, the exercitant should consider as frequently as possible throughout the day how the most holy body of Christ our Lord stayed separated and apart from His soul, and where and how the body was buried. He should likewise consider the loneliness of Our Lady in her deep sorrow and exhaustion; and too, for their part, that of the disciples.

[209] Note. It should be noted that anyone who wants to spend more time on the Passion needs to cover fewer events in each of his contemplations. To be explicit: in the first contemplation, just the Supper; in the second, only the washing of the feet; in the third, the institution of the Holy Eucharist; in the fourth, the discourse that Christ gave them; and so on through the other contemplations and saving events.

In this same way, after he has gone through the events of the Passion, he takes one whole day on one half of it, a second day on the other half, and a third day on the whole of the Passion. On the other hand, if someone wants to spend less time on the Passion: At midnight, he takes the Supper; in the morning, the Garden; around Mass time, events at the house of Annas; around Vespers, at the house of Caiaphas; and instead of the application of the senses before the evening meal, he takes events at the house of Pilate. In this way, omitting the repetitions and the application of the senses, the exercitant makes five distinct Exercises, taking for each one a different saving event in Christ our Lord's life.

After he has finished the whole Passion in this way, he might go through the entire Passion on one other day, in a single Exercise or in several, depending on what seems to him to promise more profit.

✤  **Comment 16**  ✤

# The First Set of Norms

Perhaps because the church has always connected fasting with prayer on Jesus' Passion, Ignatius puts as the added material in the Third Week some Norms for putting good order into our appetite for food and drink. Of course, your director would have known about these Norms before you began the Exercises and may have given them to you earlier on. On the other hand, some directors make little use of them.

As their title indicates, Ignatius proposes that these Norms be included among the decisions you make during your Exercises. For if you accept the gift of deep metanoia, you will have a different perspective on the ordinary things of daily life and value and even perceive them differently. Food and drink are the most ordinary of ordinary things: How will your attitude, likes, habits concerning food and drink change? These Norms suggest some lines for your decisions in this question.

To understand the Norms, you need to be aware that men and women who made the Exercises most generously under Ignatius's guidance would have been fasting and abstaining during these days. Pierre Favre, one of the first Companions, went six days without eating (Ignatius then instructed him to eat). A recent exercitant went several days without food and kept the strictest diet through the Second and Third Weeks, as any serious exercitant does. Perhaps it is not surprising that these Norms make the greatest sense to those who have already been observing the fourth Norm [213].

In some ways, the first four Norms and the last two (the seventh and eighth) make considerably fewer demands than do popular diets with their calories, food groups, and ounces. But in one way, they demand very much more: They do not call for a temporary restraint on the way you satisfy yourself, for the sake of vanity or physical health. Rather, they call for a permanent change in the way you think of and appreciate food and drink. Simply stated, they recommend that you eat solely and simply to be adequately nourished and find joy in that instead of in the savor of thyme or the richness of lemon meringue. This attitude trivializes diets and contradicts current popular culture. Here is the ground for the connection with the Last Supper and Jesus Christ's choice of bread and wine to hold in symbol and in truth the One who comes to redeem His people.

The fifth and sixth Norms put eating and drinking into the context of imitating Jesus of Nazareth. You will appreciate them better if you keep in mind that by this point in the Exercises, Ignatius expected a person to have a deep personal devotion to Jesus. We seem instinctively to imitate the manners and mores of those whom we admire greatly enough: Spaniards began lisping because the king lisped, pronouncing the letter *c* as a *th*, and American males switched from undershirts to T-shirts because a movie idol wore them. This is an instance of how, in the passionate desire to find God, Ignatius made use of everything, perhaps with an intensity not ordinary today.

## ✤ Ignatian Text ✤

[210]

# Norms about Good Order in Eating for the Future

First Norm. The first Norm: There is less need to abstain from bread, because it is not a food that stirs our appetite to the point of disorder or that provokes insistent temptation, the way some other foods do.

Second Norm. The second Norm is about drink: There seems [211] to be more need for abstinence than is the case with bread. Hence, what proves helpful should be carefully noted so as to be allowed; and what proves harmful, so as to be avoided.

Third Norm. The third Norm is about foods prepared in the [212] kitchen: Here there needs to be greater and more complete abstinence. For in this case, the appetite promptly tends just as much to excess as temptation tends to insistence. Abstinence to avoid disorder in taking prepared foods can be practiced in two ways:

First, by habitually eating the plainer foods.

Second, by eating only small amounts of more nicely prepared foods.

Fourth Norm. Provided care is taken against getting sick, the [213] more one cuts back from his ordinarily adequate diet, the more readily will he find the mean that he ought to keep in eating and drinking. There are two reasons for this: First, because as he goes forward and disposes himself this way, he will quite commonly better experience insights, consolations, and divine inspirations that will show him the mean he should follow;

Second, because if he sees that this much abstinence leaves him without enough bodily strength or energies for the Spiritual Exercises, he can easily come to determine what serves his bodily sustenance better.

Fifth Norm. The fifth Norm, he applies while eating. He might [214] imagine that he watches Christ our Lord eating with His disciples. He should consider how He drinks, how He looks around, how He converses, and then try to imitate Him. In this way, he will focus his mind mostly on considering Christ our Lord and less on nourishing his body. So he comes to more serious manners and system in the way he behaves and conducts himself.

Sixth Norm. The sixth Norm also applies while eating. He could [215] set himself at other times to ponder other things: about the life of the saints, or about some pious consideration, or about some spiritual project he has in hand. For when a person is attending to things like this, he will rest less in the sensible pleasure of his bodily food.

Seventh Norm. The seventh: Above all, he should keep himself [216] from getting completely engrossed in what he is eating and from being driven by sheer appetite to eat fast. He must at each moment keep self-mastery, just as much in the way he eats as in how much he eats.

[217]     Eighth Norm. The eighth Norm, about getting rid of some disorder. It is very useful to decide for himself immediately after having his noon or evening meal — or at some other time when the appetite for food does not make itself felt — how much to eat for the next lunch or dinner. It is useful, moreover, to do this regularly each day. He should keep to the amount he decided on, no matter how much his appetite or some temptation would take him beyond it. Instead, so as to overcome every disordered appetite and every temptation of the enemy, when he is tempted to eat more, he will eat less.

✦  Comment 17  ✦

# Ending the Third Week

Francis of Assisi received the stigmata of Christ's Passion in 1224, the first person known to have them (unless St. Paul's were physical). Since that event, perhaps three hundred others have borne the stigmata, which suggests how deeply Franciscan devotion to the sufferings of Jesus has influenced the church in the West. The devotion produced Franciscan hymns like the Stabat Mater and introduced vividly realistic paintings and sculptures of Jesus' agonies, never before acceptable, like those of Jan van Eyck and Donatello. It deepened the thirst for pilgrimage to the Holy Land and reached permanent expression in the Way of the Cross.

By the century of Ignatius's birth, the church was filled with devotion to Jesus' sufferings, in portrait and song, liturgy and spirituality. Great Dominicans like Tauler and Suso, leaders of the *devotio moderna* in the century of Ignatius's birth, considered praying the Passion the height of contemplation. Thomas à Kempis, among many others, urged constant meditation on the Passion as a source of steadiness and strength in the interior life (whence the line in the prayer Ignatius cherished, the Anima Christi, "Passion of Christ, strengthen me.")

You experience a specific strengthening during the Third Week as you go through Jesus' experience of His Passion. Within your actual set of issues and concerns, it is the strengthening of your freedom in necessity.

You brought to this prayer on the Passion from the earlier Weeks a knowledge of the demands, almost the absolutes, that your life and your world have laid into you. You know — in war, poisoned ecology, your intelligence level, your sex, and all those things that you never chose and cannot change — something of what God wants in you and the limits God has put into your freedom. In finding your most authentic desires, you have found in yourself what at once frees you and makes peremptory demands on you. "It's who I am," one woman said about the election she had made of a difficult, selfless way of life, a way she had elected in wonderful freedom.

She had followed Jesus, who both freely chose to undergo His Passion and also submitted to some kind of necessity to do so. Jesus said, it is true, "No one takes [my life] from me; I lay it down of my own free will." But He also asked, "Was it not ordained that the Christ should suffer and so enter into His glory?"

Experiencing the Passion with Jesus and as His friend, you have felt the inward weight of the question [197]: "Also to wonder, What ought I do and undergo for Him?" You are considerably more clear about what you ought to do and must not do, about what options lie open to you. And having offered the suffering Savior your election, choices, and decisions, you will begin to sense how you have fulfilled His hopes in you so far and how far you are prepared to meet His hopes still to come.

# Fourth Week

=== ✚ ===

### ✦ Comment 18 ✦

# Entering into the Joy of the Lord

Your compassion with Jesus in His test has proved, in some measure, how wholehearted and loving you have been in your election, choice, or decisions. Now you turn to rejoice in Jesus' resurrected life, continuing to sense whether your election, choice, or decisions find God's approval.

Commonly, you spend three or four days on this Week, or as many weeks in the Exercises at home. You pray only four hours a day, beginning in the early morning [227]. You throw open windows, bring flowers into your room, light candles — whatever is possible and helps. You are also likely to take greater liberty in deciding what points to touch on in prayer, and your director will do little more than suggest Scripture passages [228]. He is likely to remind you of the points added to the usual three in this Week, as they were in the Third Week. Ignatius suggests a fourth point, how Jesus now manifests His divinity as once he hid it, and a fifth, how He comes to His friends to bring consolation and not to look for it.

The gift you ask is to enter into the joy of the Lord. Entering into another's joy is not an everyday concept, but you can grasp it readily. Imagine that you are tone-deaf and do not like music. But you have a friend who wins a role in an operetta. You are delighted for your friend. You attend the performance on opening night. Your friend is loudly applauded by everyone. You feel keen happiness and applaud until your hands hurt although you caught none of the music at all. You just rejoice at your friend's achievement. You have *entered into the joy* of your friend.

Jesus of Nazareth, dead and buried, driven out of our flesh, rose again to human life. He has won His victory. He has conquered suffering, death, and their source, sin. He has the infinite joy of knowing that He will share this risen life with His friends. You know nothing about resurrection, but you can watch Him as He comes to friends, you among them. So you enter into this joy of Jesus. You had been asking before His suffering and death to know Him, love Him, and follow Him. Now you find the final truth: He goes into joy.

This is why Ignatius included the Fourth Week in the Spiritual Exercises. If you have honestly begun to follow Jesus Christ and have gone with Him into the demands made by your God-given self and gifts and by the life world into which God summons you to live, then you will indeed find joy. You do not make yourself joyful; you find your joy. Joy is, Thomas Aquinas contends, the immediate glow and warmth of the love of God accepted. Hence, should you not be able to find the joy of the Lord who promised that "your hearts will be full of joy and that joy no one shall take from you" (John 16:22), then you need to wonder whether you have found as yet what God hopes in you, whether you really have begun to imitate Jesus Christ. The Fourth Week, in brief, is an integral part of the confirmation of your election or choice.

In the contemplations, you follow Him first to the room where His mother waited. Ignatius, very careful in his use of Scripture, allowed that this event is not explicitly mentioned, though we all know it happened. More than one exercitant has heard the Lady Mary say, "I knew you would come." Then, one by one, you go through the wonderful confusion of the apparitions — everyone telling everyone else who saw Jesus first — to the Ascension. For reasons we do not know, Ignatius did not include Pentecost; your director may or may not.

### The Contemplation to Reach Love

At the end of the materials on the Resurrection, Ignatius includes an original contemplation, "The Contemplation to Reach Love."

You might pray through the saving events of the Resurrection and then, on the last day or two of your Exercises, turn to the "Contemplation to Reach Love." But, considering the way directors now work, you are more likely, from the second day of this Week on, to alternate a contemplation on Christ's Resurrection with an hour on the "Contemplation to Reach Love." Ignatius left no clear directive about this, and his contemporaries used both formats.

If he left no directives about its use, he did indicate its importance by asking the exercitant to compose himself or herself before the whole court of heaven (done before only in the "Three Sorts of People") and by offering the text of a Colloquy (done before only in "The Call of the King").

Ignatius begins this contemplation with an unusual and characteristic note. Before you begin, he suggests, be mindful of two things about love: Love is in deeds, not in words; and love entails constant, generous mutual sharing between lover and beloved. He here describes the way God loves, and the point of this contemplation is precisely to enter upon the way God loves.

The point is not to obtain God's love, or to learn to love God. It is to know how to love the way God loves, and to love God and every other person in that way.

Ignatius gives four points on how God loves: God gives gifts; God remains present in the gifts and in yourself, who are also a gift; God keeps acting in and through those gifts, including yourself; God shares the divine Self, giving and receiving. You are uniting yourself with the beloved not for the sake of the union, but for the sake of finding out what the beloved has in mind to do and of doing it with the beloved. When Ignatius spoke on other occasions about "finding God in all things," he did not mean finding a Presence or a quiet communion only; he meant finding God acting and creating.

Ignatius draws on the Augustinian tradition in this prayer form, in which reasoning plays a large role. You will reason through these topics, considering the whole globe and your whole life world and all your own gifts. You face the temptation of getting lost in the universe; you resist it by listing your own agenda — the great desires God has raised in your spirit, the election or choice you have taken, the concrete helps and obstacles you have grown keenly aware of — among the gifts God has lavished on you.

You have come back to the start, gratitude. Now, however, besides knowing how many gifts you have been given and how God's merciful love has chosen you specially, you also hope you know what of your desiring rises out of God's love and what out of some other source, world or flesh or evil. You have grounds to hope that your own specific elections, choices, and decisions are also gifts of God's love. So when you say the prayer Ignatius writes for this contemplation, you are asking God to take and receive your own specific desires, concrete determinations, and limited and scarred liberty.

There is no joy like knowing that Jesus Christ finds you acceptable and more than acceptable. You, the person that you are, not the person that you might have been, or could be, or ought to be. This divine exchange of love goes on every moment, every now.

## ❖ Ignatian Text ❖

# The Resurrection of Jesus Christ

### [218] First Contemplation

*How Christ our Lord appeared to Our Lady.*

Readiness Prayer. The Readiness Prayer will be the same.

[219]   First Prelude. The first Prelude is the salvation story. After Christ died on the cross, His body stayed apart from His soul but always united with His divinity. His holy soul, also always united with His divinity, went down into the underworld and from it freed the souls of the just. Returning to the tomb and rising again, He appeared body and soul to His Blessed Mother.

[220]   Second Prelude. The second Prelude is to compose myself in the place. Here I regard the arrangement of the holy sepulchre and then the place or house of Our Lady, noting in detail its various parts, such as her chamber, her oratory, and the rest.

[221]   Third Prelude. The third Prelude is to ask for what I want. Now

it will be to ask for the grace to rejoice with a keen joy because of the great glory and joy of Christ our Lord.

First, Second, and Third Points. These three points would be [222] the usual ones as detailed in the Last Supper of Christ our Lord.

Fourth Point. The fourth point is to consider how His divinity, [223] which seemed to hide itself during the Passion, now shows and manifests itself miraculously in the most holy Resurrection by its true and most holy results.

Fifth Point. The fifth point is to consider the ministry of consol- [224] ing that Christ our Lord undertakes, and to compare it with the ways friends follow in consoling one another.

Colloquy. Finish with a Colloquy or Colloquies, according to [225] the subject matter, and an Our Father.

### Notes

First Note. The exercitant will proceed in the following contem- [226] plations through all of the events after the Resurrection down to and including the Ascension, in the way indicated just below. In all other matters during the Week of the Resurrection, the method followed and the forms used will be the same as they were in the Week of the Passion.

This first contemplation on the Resurrection sets the model: The Preludes are to be the same, adapted to the subject matter; the five points are to be the same; the Additions given below will be the same. In everything else, the procedures of the Week of the Passion can be taken as a guide: the repetitions, the application of the senses, shortening or lengthening the saving events considered, and the rest.

Second Note. As a general rule, it is more in keeping with the [227] Fourth Week than with the other three to make four Exercises a day instead of five. The first will be right after getting up in the morning; the second, around Mass time or before the noon meal, in place of the first repetition; the third, around the time of Vespers, in place of the second repetition; and the fourth, which will be the application of the senses to the day's Exercises, before the evening meal. In this Exercise, he should mark out and dwell on the main places where he felt moved more noticeably and savored stronger spiritual experiences.

Third Note. Though for each contemplation a fixed number of [228] points is given, such as three or five, the person contemplating can propose more or fewer for himself, as he finds better. In this matter, he will find it very useful to have estimated which points he ought to take up and to have set a definite number before going into the contemplation.

[229] Fourth Note. Of the ten Additions, the second, sixth, seventh, and tenth need adjusting during this Fourth Week.

The second will be: As soon as I wake up, I focus my mind on the contemplation I am about to make, trying to rejoice and to feel delight at the great joy and happiness of Christ our Lord.

The sixth will be to call to mind and think about things that bring pleasure, cheerfulness, and spiritual delight, such as the glories of heaven.

The seventh will be to use light or the pleasant things about the season — fresh coolness in the summer, the warmth of the sun or of a fire in the winter — to the extent that the person believes or estimates that it will help toward rejoicing in his Creator and Lord.

The tenth will be: Instead of penitential practices, he should attend to temperance and moderation in everything — unless this is on days of fast and abstinence prescribed by the church, which are always to be observed if there is no legitimate excuse.

## [230] Contemplation to Reach Love

Note: To begin with, it helps to note two things:

The first is that love has to set about doing deeds rather than saying things.

[231] The second is that love consists in mutual sharing on both sides. So the lover gives to and shares with the beloved what he has — or something out of what he has or is able to give — and the beloved in turn does the same for the lover. And so it goes: If one has knowledge, he gives it to the other, or honor, or wealth. And the other acts in the same way.

Readiness Prayer. The Readiness Prayer as usual.

[232] First Prelude. The first Prelude is to compose myself in the place. Here I will see myself standing before God our Lord and before His angels and saints, who are interceding for me.

[233] Second Prelude. The second Prelude is to ask for what I want. Now, it will be for an interior knowledge of all the great good I have been given, so that I might acknowledge to the

fullest the whole of it and be able to love and serve His Divine Majesty.

First Point. The first point is to call to mind the favors I have [234] received in creation and in redemption and in my concrete gifts. I will ponder with deep feeling how much God our Lord has done for me, and how much He has given to me of what He has. Everything suggests that this same Lord of mine wishes to give Himself to me as far as He can according to His divine design.

Then I reflect about myself. I consider what, for excellent reason and in justice, I ought to offer and give to the Divine Majesty for my part — plainly, everything I have and myself with it. Then I ought to offer as one moved by the deepest affection:

> Take, Lord, and receive all my liberty, my memory, my understanding, and my entire will — all I have and all I possess. You have given it to me; I return it, Lord, to You. Everything is Yours; dispose of all according to Your will. Give me Your love and Your grace; for me, that is enough.

Second Point. I consider how God dwells in His creatures: in [235] the elements, giving them being; in plants, giving them life; in animals, sensation; in humans, understanding. And so He dwells in me and gives me existence, life, sensation, understanding. More, He makes a temple of me, since I am created in the image and likeness of His Divine Majesty.

Once again I reflect about myself in the way given in the first point or in some way I feel is better.

This same procedure will be followed in each of the points given below.

Third Point. I consider how God toils and labors for me in all [236] created things on the face of the earth — as the learned say, "He conducts Himself after the manner of one who labors." So again, in the heavens, in the elements, in plants, fruits, flocks, and in everything else, He gives existence, preserves, makes grow, gives sensation, and so on.

Afterward I reflect about myself.

Fourth Point. I consider the way all good gifts descend from [237] above. Thus, my limited power comes from the supreme and infinite power above, and so with justice, goodness, devotion, mercy, and the rest. It is the way rays come from the sun, or waters from a wellspring, or so on.

Afterward I will finish by reflecting about myself, as has been said.

End with a Colloquy and an Our Father.

✤ **Comment 19** ✤

# Three More Ways to Pray

While he was helping a person learn to pray during the Exercises, Ignatius was preparing her or him to continue afterward. You remember that he strongly recommended continuing the daily Examen of Conscience throughout life. He also hoped that the contemplations would afford an introduction and method for better and more complete meditation later, after the month or months were over [162].

As the added materials in the Fourth Week, he included directions for some further ways of praying. The first and most affective, judging by its title, Ignatius seems to have considered part of the long quiet of the Exercises, the "Contemplation to Reach Love." The three others Ignatius calls "forms" or "methods" of prayer, categories that include meditation and contemplation, but explains that he means something much simpler, like a "technique." He left little indication about their use, but appears to have found them useful for simple people and in everyday life, and in fact composed the paragraphs early on, while he was helping souls at Manresa with the Examen of Conscience.

He may well have recommended these ways to persons he was guiding through the whole of the Exercises (perhaps the first Annotation suggests that), but left no instructions on the point. His contemporaries considered the first of the added three ways as a part of the "light" Exercises, those parts of Spiritual Exercises that they gave to people with little education or spiritual desires. Your director may have suggested that you use one or other of these ways of praying between your hours of prayer and may call your attention to them as helpful in everyday life.

The first method reflects the taste in Ignatius's day for lists and catalogues. He suggests that you take each item in a list and examine yourself on it, pray over what you discover, and then pass on to the next. He suggests four different lists: First, the Commandments. Second, the Seven Capital Sins: pride, covetousness, lust, envy, anger, gluttony, and sloth; and the opposing virtues, which can be listed this way: humility, generosity, chastity, fellow-feeling, patience, temperance, and initiative. Third, the three powers of the soul: memory, understanding, and free will. Fourth, the five senses of our enfleshed self: sight, taste, touch, smell, and hearing.

The second method of prayer seems related to *lectio divina*, the prayerful consideration of the Scripture that reaches back into Old Testament times. Ignatius is suggesting that the illiterate and those who have no access to the Bible at the moment might still use this method. Simply take as a text the Our Father or some other common prayer known by heart.

The third method is akin to the Jesus Prayer insofar as it is the rhythmic repetition of a word or words. Unlike the mantra or the Jesus Prayer, however, this method moves the one praying along through the texts of ordinary prayers. It could hardly move you into a wordless prayer, but it achieves a similar self-concentration or centering.

Ignatius wrote no instructions about when or how to use these prayers except an oblique remark about the second method that a person who uses it might go through various prayers over a period of days, "so that for a while he is constantly exercising himself in one of them" [256].

✤ **Ignatian Text** ✤

# [238] Three Methods of Praying

### First Method

*This first way to pray is on the Ten Commandments, the Seven Capital Sins, the soul's three powers, and the five senses.*

Note. This *method* simply lays out a format — a way of proceeding and some practices — by which a person can prepare for and realize some profit, and make his prayer more pleasing to God. It is not strictly a Form of Prayer, or a Method.

*I. On the Ten Commandments*

[239] Addition. First of all, the equivalent of the second Addition as given in the Second Week should be done. And so, before going into prayer, I come to self-concentration for a little while. I might be sitting or pacing up and down, whichever seems better. I consider where I am going and for what.

This same directive should be kept at the beginning of each of these methods of praying.

[240] Prayer. A preparatory prayer should be said. For example, I would ask God our Lord for the gift of knowing how I have failed to keep the Ten Commandments and also for the grace to help amend for the future. I beg for a thorough understanding of them in order to obey them better for the greater glory and praise of His Divine Majesty.

[241] Format. To pray in this first way, I would consider and think over the First Commandment, how I have kept it and how I have failed, staying with the reflection about as long as it takes to say three Our Fathers and three Hail Marys. If during this time I find faults I have committed, I beg forgiveness and pardon for them. Then I say the Our Father. This same procedure should be used on each one of the Ten Commandments.

[242] Note I. This should be noted: When a person comes to the consideration of a commandment against which he has no habit of

sinning, he need not dwell on it long. So, depending on whether he sins more or less against a given commandment, he would spend more or less time considering and examining it. He would do the same with the capital sins.

Note II. After having made this reckoning for every one of the [243] commandments, blaming myself for failing in them, and begging the grace to help amend myself in the future, I end with a Colloquy with God our Lord according to the subject matter.

## II. On the Capital Sins [244]

Format. To pray on the Seven Capital Sins: After making the Addition, he should make a preparatory prayer as it was described. He should change it only in that the matter here involves sins to be avoided, while the matter there involved commandments to be kept. He should also follow the same procedure, measure of time, and Colloquy.

Note. In order to know better the failings that are catalogued [245] under the Seven Capital Sins, he needs to consider the virtues opposing them. And along the same line, to keep from falling into the seven sins, he could determine to try by devout exercises to acquire and to practice the seven virtues that are their opposites.

## III. On the Three Powers of the Soul [246]

Format. To pray on the three powers of the soul: Follow the same procedure and measure of time as on the Commandments, making the Addition, a preparatory prayer, and the Colloquy.

## IV. On the Five Senses of the Body [247]

Format. To pray on the five senses of the body: The same procedure should be followed exactly, only the subject changing.

Note. Anyone who wants to imitate Christ our Lord in the use [248] of his senses, should recommend himself to His Divine Majesty in the preparatory prayer and then, as he finishes considering each of the senses, say a Hail Mary or an Our Father.

And if someone wants to imitate Our Lady in the use of his senses, he should recommend himself to her in the preparatory prayer, asking that she obtain this gift for him from her Son and Lord, and then, as he considers each of the senses, say a Hail Mary.

**[249] Second Method**

The second way of praying is to consider the meaning of each word in a common prayer.

[250]   Addition. The same Addition that was observed in the first method will be observed in this second.

[251]   Prayer. A preparatory prayer should be formulated according to the person to whom the common prayer is addressed.

[252]   Format. In following the second method of praying, the person might kneel or sit, doing what he feels more inclined to do and what gives him more devotion. He might keep his eyes closed or fixed on one spot without glancing around.

Then he says, "Father." He should keep pondering this word as long as he finds meanings, comparisons, spiritual taste, and consolation in his thoughts about it. Then he should do the same thing with each word of the Our Father — or of any other prayer that he wants to use in this way.

[253]   Norm I. The first Norm is that he continue praying this way for an hour on the whole of the Our Father. When he has done, he should say in the ordinary way, either out loud or in his mind, the Hail Mary, the Creed, the Anima Christi, and the Hail Holy Queen.

[254]   Norm II. The second Norm is that if someone meditating on the Our Father finds in one or two words plenty of meaning, spiritual taste, and consolation, he need not feel anxious to move along, even though he use the whole hour on what he finds. When his time is up, he ought to finish saying the Our Father in the ordinary way.

[255]   Norm III. The third Norm applies when he has spent a whole hour on one or two words of the Our Father and on another day wants to go back to it. Then he might just say that word or those words in the ordinary way and when he comes to the very next word, he can begin to contemplate, careful to follow the second Norm.

[256]   Note I. This should be noted: After he has done with the Our Father in one or more days, he might well use the Hail Mary for praying in the same way, and then other prayers, so that for a while he is constantly exercising himself in one of them.

[257]   Note II. A second note: When he comes to the end of the prayer, he should turn to the one to whom it is directed and, in a few words, beg for the virtues or the gifts that he senses he needs most.

## Third Method [258]

*This is a method using rhythmic recitation.*

Addition. The Addition will be the same as in the first and the second methods of praying.

Prayer. A preparatory prayer will be just like that in the second method.

Format. In this third way of praying, the person prays mentally by saying a single word of a prayer — the Our Father or any other that he wants to pray — while breathing in and out. During that one breath, he would focus mainly on the meaning of that one word, or on the person to whom it is spoken, or on his own lowliness, or on the difference between such greatness and his own littleness. So, keeping this same procedure and rhythm, he would go through the other words of the Our Father, or of the other prayers usually recited, like the Hail Mary, Anima Christi, Creed, and the Hail Holy Queen.

Norm I. The first Norm is that when someone wants to pray [259] this way on another day, or at another time on the same day, he might recite the Hail Mary in this rhythmic way and the rest in the ordinary way. Using this method, he might go through all of the common prayers in sequence.

Norm II. The second Norm applies to someone who wants to [260] keep at this rhythmic prayer for a rather long time. He might say all of the prayers mentioned or any part of them. But he should keep his breathing as a rhythmic measure.

# Added Materials
# for the Director

═══ ✛ ═══

✤ **Comment 20** ✤

# Scripture Passages and Points

After all of the materials for the Four Weeks, Ignatius added what we would call an appendix. The first of its five items gives the "points" on the saving events of Jesus' life that have been referred to [2]. These bare outlines helped people who had no Bible; they are not much used now. They give no hint of the richness of the prayer they lead to and even make that richness hard to imagine. Hence, they are not printed here. For during the Exercises, exercitants use these points in various ways and for various methods. You will understand the *Spiritual Exercises* better if you remember these methods of prayer.

*Praying with Fantasy.* In fantasizing, you experience things that have not and perhaps could not happen. You did this in the meditation on "The Call of the King." You may well be doing it when you contemplate, say, the Flight into Egypt. Fantasy opens horizons and often leads to action. A boy fantasizes parachuting enough times and ends up jumping out of a tree. Francis Xavier fantasized going to India, again and again; when Ignatius suddenly asked him to go, he answered instantly, "Listen! Yes! I'm your man."

*Prayer of Consideration.* When Ignatius suggests that you consider, he suggests a kind of prayer that engages understanding and reason most of all. It is in the tradition of St. Augustine. In God's presence, you quietly analyze an event or a text, take it apart, and question what it tells about your life. You let it move you and motivate you, clarifying faith and sharpening hope, and turn to God with what you find. Actually, this way of praying seems to be very ordinary in everyday life, and does indeed play a large role in the Exercises at home.

During the Exercises, you deliberately take to the prayer of consideration your lifestyle and some habits and attitudes you are choosing to curtail or to strengthen. You also consider, at Ignatius's urging, how Jesus hid His divinity, how a person can lose himself or herself in sin, how to live humbly, and so on. It is one of the characteristics of Ignatian praying that you do not move away from active intelligence but readily turn to thinking and reasoning.

*Meditation.* Meditating is a way of praying through salvation events like Jesus' baptism or His arrest. You meditate by remembering a real event in true detail, as though you were a camera taking in all the action, always ready to focus in tightly. Great theologians like Bonaventure used it, as their writings show, and the ancient Fathers like Basil share its results when they explain the spiritual meaning of the Scriptures. When you meditate, you "reflect upon these things to find some good for myself," as Ignatius constantly reminds you. Ordinarily, you can say definitely what you have prayed about after you meditate, for this prayer tends to images and explicit feelings and stays close to words.

*Contemplation.* Teresa of Avila and others were given a gift of prayer called "infused contemplation." They are hard pressed to tell what this prayer is like because ordinary words or images cannot match their experience. A very few men and women going through the Spiritual Exercises have given evidence of this kind of prayer (Teresa herself prayed through the First Week). However, it is not the contemplation typical of the Spiritual Exercises.

The contemplation you do during the Exercises grows from the exercise of our memory and imagination as they have been charged with the graces of faith, hope, and love. You are usually active in this kind of contemplation and sometimes you are aware of having to work at it (recall the "strive with all my might" of the Third Week). But though you use memory and imagination, you do not remain a spectator but become an actor in the event. You not only observe what is done and hear what is said, you take part in it. One man exclaimed after Jesus' baptism: "I was there! I was in it! I didn't just see it." You experience the dynamism of the event, what Gerard Manley Hopkins would call its "inscape," of thoughts and feelings and wishes. You enter into the spirit of the actors. This prayer is itself an experience, real and often enough unforgettable. Commonly, you come away from it with the strong memory of a gesture or a word or a feeling. You might be able to tell about it, but what you say will be a hopelessly poor reflection of what you experienced.

*The Application of the Senses.* You have already met this way of praying. It is probably best thought of as a kind of contemplation, known in the church long before Ignatius's time. It is a simple way of attending corporeally to a salvation event, by letting each physical sense report its experience after you have spent considerable time on a saving event. It is a quiet and simple kind of prayer that tends to make our spirits quiet and simple.

In the course of the Four Weeks, Ignatius calls for the use of imagination, consideration, meditation, and contemplation in various exercises. You will not often have felt concern to name which of these methods you were using, however, nor will you have been asked by your director which way you are praying unless you have hit a particularly difficult period and she or he has followed the sixth Annotation and inquired how you were proceeding. Most exercitants begin the Exercises doing the prayer of consideration and grow through meditation into contemplation as they go further into the silence and aloneness of the thirty days. Often enough, those who make the Exercises at home, provided only they pray long enough each day, go through the same growth. Generally, however, consideration and meditation belong to every day and contemplation belongs to retirement and stillness.

✦ **Comment 21** ✦

# Four Sets of Norms

Ignatius gathered into the book's appendix, after the points on Jesus' life, four series of Norms. Three of them are not translated here because they are no longer used and call for elaborate historical explanation: on managing benefices, on scruples, and on appreciating the church during the Reformation. The final set, however, continues in use and is important for the experience of the Exercises: "Norms Followed in Discerning Spirits."

The discernment of spirits preoccupied Ignatius from the beginning of his interior life. For he began that life when he noticed that he felt different after daydreaming over chivalric romances than he felt after reading the life of Christ or of the saints. After he had made his confession and lived penitentially for several months, he had the great illumination at the River Cardoner. Then, he said, "he began to see everything with different eyes, and to distinguish and experience good and evil spirits." He also began to share his experience with others and learn from their experiences.

What did he see so differently? What are the issues involved in "discernment"? Ignatius begins with the fundamental issue of recognizing sin and temptation to sin. But he moves beyond that to junctures where conscience remains silent but choices must be made. For instance, how much prayer is enough? too much? And how much penance, and study, and work for others? How can I ensure that my intention to put God first stays real? Does a particular natural instinct that I am moved by lead to holiness, or will it lead me merely into the earth's cycle of life? Does this or that inspiration come from God, or from somewhere else (noble humanism, my own subconscious)?

Such issues, as you have seen, rise at every juncture during the experience of the Spiritual Exercises. At their very beginning, Ignatius noted that the one going through the Exercises ought to feel consolation and desolation and the movements of various spirits [6, 17]. He collected some information on the movement of spirits in the notes on election at the end of the Second Week [169–89]. Actually, Ignatius constantly calls for discernment in Preludes, notes, and Colloquies. Whether to pray at midnight would be one instance [129], and whether you can honestly pray to imitate Jesus in humility would be another [168].

Ignatius put these Norms together over a period of about twenty-five years, so they record what he learned from his experience of disparate peoples. The earliest of these paragraphs, the fifth through the fourteenth Norms of the first set on discerning spirits [318–27], he wrote while working in Manresa with men and women just converting from sin and carelessness to an interior life. He simply states in these Norms things to do and not do, as he was learning from his own conversion and from helping others as a lay apostle. Later on in Paris, conversing with people trained in theology and philosophy, he found it useful to write out a clear description of spiritual consolation and desolation [316, 317].

Once the Companions finished their absorbing studies in Paris, they gave themselves eagerly to apostolic work. In Venice, in the dead of winter of 1537, they began giving every kind of Spiritual Exercises. They preached to the illiterate, catechized, and brought people back to the sacraments. They found devout people — two bishops, a new Companion, and a future pope among them — and invited them through the Spiritual Exercises. Banking on his more than fifteen years' experience and responding to this broadening of ministry, Ignatius described how spirits move differently in the careless and in the committed [314–15]. It was here in Venice, a city known for its surpluses and luxuries, that he wrote the Norms for discerning how to eat and drink that you have read in the materials for the Third Week.

In Rome, where they had all gathered by the end of 1538, Ignatius and the Companions began to work in parishes and with the Roman establishment. Then the Companions scattered all over Italy and became more involved with religious in monasteries and convents. For them, Ignatius wrote the last set of Norms he would complete, those for the more advanced discernment of spirits in the Second Week [328–36].

## The Many Meanings of "Spirits"

Spiritual writers and theologians long before Ignatius had discoursed on the discernment or discretion of spirits. St. Bernard in the twelfth century and John Gerson in the fourteenth produced works that had widespread influence; and Denis the Carthusian, who died twenty years before Ignatius's birth, put order into this spiritual doctrine. Ignatius certainly learned from them — St. Bernard, for instance, first made the commonplace comparison of the devil to an angry woman [325] — but we do not know how or how much.

By "spirit" writers have meant many things. They have meant first of all a larger mindset or *Weltanschauung* marked by characteristic perspectives, values, decisions, and habits. Understand: They have not meant theoretical constructs or ideas, but rather concrete forces whose work we can see and experience. In this sense, ancient writers spoke of the spirit of the world, of the flesh, and of the devil. We use this same sense in a rather diminished way when we talk about "school spirit" or the Marine "esprit de corps."

We tend to think that we do not personify these forces, which may indeed be the case. The authors of Scripture, however, surely did. They personified evil in the person of the Liar. Some of them also plainly believed that the messengers of the good God are personified as angels, and the Opponent's messengers as devils. The church in Ignatius's day, including the Protestants, held a firm belief in angels and devils.

Writers since the historical books of the Old Testament use the term "spirit" in another sense, to refer to movements within yourself, and talk about a spirit moving you or preventing you. Thus, Saul was seized by a spirit of jealousy toward David. In the earlier books, God sends both good and evil spirits of this kind upon His chosen ones; but later on, an opposition develops between the good, which comes from God, and the evil, which comes from the Opponent. This development came to a culmination of sorts in the Gospel of John, which so insistently opposes the spirits of Light and Dark, of Life and Death.

As this development unfolded in the church of Ignatius's time, Christians were convinced that they were following Scripture in their perception that personal spirits were inspiring and moving men and women all the time. They felt little speculative curiosity about how the diverse spirits achieved this or what its implication might be to human freedom. Theologians and churchmen in particular were forced to a more practical interest in these spirits because they had to deal with many people who were experiencing visions and revelations and who were prophesying from some inner light.

Ignatius evinced no such interests. He was interested in these spirits, rather, because of their influence on an individual's actions and attitudes, and because the spirits indicate a person's interior dispositions. His Norms do not test the orthodoxy of a belief or help extirpate heresies. He meant them to guide action under grace and to identify action's sources in the movements of our minds and hearts. When does feeling good lead to God and when away from God? How do you know whether to trust an inspiration to do something? These are the movements addressed by Ignatius's Norms.

One reflection, mentioned earlier, has grown more important as more Christians talk about discernment. Ignatian discernment results not in clarity of belief or in certitude, but in hopeful enactment. It is a process through which you try to determine whether the development of a thought or commitment proves that it began in God or began somewhere else, and whether a course of action will lead you to God or lead somewhere else.

## Norms for Discerning Spirits

The first set of Norms, "For the First Week," refract the experience of people who are struggling to get free of sin. Ignatius recognized a basic difference in the spiritual experiences of those still struggling out of sin and of those already deeply committed to God in Christ. These first Norms detail how good and bad spirits influence the thought, feeling, and action of the first group struggling out of sin.

The distinction that Ignatius makes between consolation and desolation may be taken as traditional, but has a clarity and succinctness not reached by earlier spiritual writers [316, 317]. It has become standard, though you might note that it is not the same distinction that John of the Cross introduces in his reflections on the dark night of the senses and of the soul.

The last three Norms in this set suggest metaphors that have proven useful in comprehending patterns in the movements of spirits among those who struggle with sin [325–27]. Ignatius compares the evil spirit's way of proceeding to the shadow side of the *anima* (the female wants things different) and of the *animus* (the male wants dominion), and describes his tactics in military terms. Directors now use these illustrations carefully.

The second part of these Norms, "For the Second Week," help people who are seriously giving themselves to the Exercises and deeply committed to the spiritual life. These Norms would confuse beginners, as Ignatius mentioned in Annotation 9, but they help those who have gone far enough to recognize and repudiate promptly any blatant temptation to do wrong. They are necessary and necessarily more subtle because, as the fourth Norm explains, those seriously growing in the interior life will be tempted away from the good by something that seems on its face good. Ignatius had a vivid experience of this when he was trying to learn Latin in Barcelona. He would sit before his grammar book for hours, but he would be wrapped in loving contemplation of God our Lord and learn no grammar. When he realized that one good (consoling prayer) was taking him from the good he had set out to do (learn Latin so he could study theology), he had discovered an important lesson about how the spirit of evil persists.

The subtlety of doctrine embodied in these Norms emerges in what Ignatius, in what seems an original insight, calls "consolation without any previous cause" [330]. He means that you are seized by a notable illumination, strengthening, or determination in a moment when you are doing nothing to occasion or evoke the consolation. The most recent theological opinion, expressed clearly by Karl Rahner, holds that this is the actual experience of God working directly on our selves. The subtlety of the experiences addressed by the second part of these Norms is clear in Ignatius's observation about decisions taken in later stages of a consolation [336].

These Norms for discernment were much taught and written about in the decades after Ignatius's death. They are used a good deal today, and a considerable literature has grown up around them. You will notice when you read them that Ignatius does not discourse at all on theology, for instance on how grace moves our free will without determining it or on how evil inhabits our selves. He is writing Norms that are useful in deciding where a desire or attitude comes from and where it leads, and in determining how to act.

## ✤ Ignatian Text ✤

# Norms Followed [313]
# in Discerning Spirits

### I. For the First Week

*Norms for perceiving and, at least to some extent, comprehending diverse movements caused in the soul, to accept the good ones and to reject the bad ones. These Norms are more suitable to the First Week.*

First Norm. In the case of those who go from one mortal sin to [314] another: The enemy usually proposes to them apparent pleasures. He fills their imagination with sensual gratifications and delights in order to keep them fixed in their vices and sins and to make them worse. With this kind of person, the good spirit follows a procedure the reverse of that. By stirring up their seasoned moral judgment, the good spirit pricks their consciences and fills them with remorse.

Second Norm. In the case of persons who are seriously pu- [315] rifying themselves of their sins and who are growing in God's service from good to better, the procedures reverse those of the first Norm.

Now it is characteristic of the evil spirit to evoke gnawing regret, to afflict with sadness, and to throw up obstacles by upsetting these persons with fallacious reasoning. All this to keep them from going ahead.

And it is characteristic of the good spirit to fill with courage and strength, consolations, tears, inspirations, and peace, making things easy and removing obstacles. All this to move the good work forward.

Third Norm. About spiritual consolation: I call it consolation [316] when some interior movement is stirred in the soul that makes a person catch fire with love of the Creator and Lord. As a result, he can love no creature on the face of the earth for its own sake, but only in the Creator of all.

Furthermore, it is consolation when someone sheds tears that move him to love the Lord — at one time they might be in sorrow for his sins; at another, over Christ our Lord's Passion; or over anything truly ordered to His service and praise. Finally, I call consolation every increase of hope, faith, and love, and all inward joy that calls and draws a person to what is heavenly and to the salvation of his own soul by quieting him and bringing him peace in his Creator and Lord.

[317]   Fourth Norm. About spiritual desolation: I call desolation whatever is the opposite of the things described in the third Norm, like darkness of soul and confusion of spirit; an instinct for low and earthly things; a restlessness brought on by all kinds of vexations and temptations. He is drawn to be faithless; he is without hope and without love. He finds himself utterly lazy, tepid, unhappy, and feels simply cut off from his Creator.

For just as consolation is the opposite of desolation, so the thoughts that rise out of consolation are the opposite of those that rise out of desolation.

[318]   Fifth Norm. The time of desolation is not the time to change the resolutions and decisions taken the day before that desolation or during a prior time of consolation. It is the time to stand firm and be constant. For as in consolation it is regularly the good spirit who guides and counsels us, so in desolation it is regularly the evil spirit who does. We never find our way to a sound decision by his counsels.

[319]   Sixth Norm. Although in desolation we should not change resolutions taken earlier, we do well to make some extensive changes in ourselves that go against that same desolation. As instances, we might insist more on prayer, on meditation, and on searching self-examination, and we can extend ourselves in doing suitable penances.

[320]   Seventh Norm. Anyone in desolation might consider how the Lord has left him to prove himself by fending off with just his natural powers the various commotions and temptations of the enemy. He can do that with divine help, which always stays with him, even if he may not sense it clearly. For though the Lord withdraw deep fervor, abounding love, and keenly felt gifts, He of course leaves grace enough to reach eternal salvation.

[321]   Eighth Norm. Anyone in desolation needs to work at being patient, which goes directly against the harassing he suffers. He might keep in mind that he will be consoled presently, and in

the interim diligently take the steps mentioned in the sixth Norm against the desolation.

Ninth Norm. The main causes why we find ourselves made [322] desolate are these three:

The first is that we are lukewarm, lazy, or careless in our spiritual exercises; so through our own fault consolation goes away.

The second is to test out what we are worth and how far we will extend ourselves in God's praise and service without such a great reward in consolation and increasing graces.

The third is to give us clear notice and knowledge, so that we reach a deeply felt sense, that we do not have the power to achieve or sustain great devotion, burning love, tears, or any other spiritual consolation. The fact is that all of these are gifts and graces from God our Lord. So desolation teaches us not to "build our nest on someone else's branch" — not to rise up in a certain pride or vain-glory and give ourselves credit for the devotion or any of the other elements in spiritual consolation.

Tenth Norm. While anyone is in consolation, he does well to [323] muse how he will act in the desolation that will come, fortifying himself for that time.

Eleventh Norm. A person given consolation needs to humble [324] and abase himself as much as he can, thinking how little he is worth in time of desolation when he goes without this grace and consolation. And just the other way around, the person in desolation needs to think that he can do a good deal with the adequate grace always given him to stand up to all his enemies, as long as he finds his strength in his Creator and Lord.

Twelfth Norm. The enemy acts like a woman, weak before main [325] strength but strong when given the initiative. For in a quarrel with a man, a woman ordinarily loses heart and retreats when he squarely confronts her. But when, on the contrary, he starts to cave in and retreat, her raging, spite, and ferocity mount and know no bounds.

It is the same with the enemy, whose nature it is to weaken and lose courage and to withdraw his temptations when the person leading a spiritual life squarely confronts these temptations, going diametrically against them. And on the contrary, when such a person begins to fear and grow disheartened under the temptations, there is no animal on the face of the earth as fierce as the enemy of human nature when he pursues his wicked designs with deepening malice.

[326]    Thirteenth Norm. A similar example: The enemy conducts himself like a false lover. He wants to stay hidden and undiscovered. For when a seducer woos the daughter of a good father or the wife of a faithful husband with lecherous talk, he wants his words and solicitations kept secret. And he is very displeased when they are not, when the daughter tells her father or the wife tells her husband about the lecherous talk and the attempted seduction. He promptly infers that he cannot succeed in the project he has begun.

In the same way, when the enemy of humankind works his wily solicitations on a committed person, he really wants them received in secret and kept secret. So the e is much vexed when they are revealed to a good confessor or to some spiritual person who is familiar with his deceits and malicious designs. He gathers that once his transparent wiles are brought to light, he cannot succeed in his wicked project.

[327]    Fourteenth Norm. Another example. The enemy conducts himself like a military leader out to make his conquest and seize his plunder. A captain fielding his army will set up his camp and explore the forces and fortifications of a citadel. He will then storm it at its weakest point.

In this same way, the enemy of humankind circles around us, probing in turn each of our theological, cardinal, and moral virtues. Where he finds us weakest and most needy in our search for eternal salvation, there he storms in and tries to take us.

### [328] II. For the Second Week

*Norms for discerning the diverse spirits with greater subtlety, which are more suitable to the Second Week.*

[329]    First Norm. The characteristic way that God and His angels act on a person is to give genuine happiness and spiritual joy by taking away every sadness and disturbance engendered by the enemy.

The characteristic way of the enemy is to struggle against that spiritual happiness and consolation by throwing up specious tangles of ideas full of subtleties and convoluted fallacies.

[330]    Second Norm. God alone can give a person consolation with-

out any previous cause. For it is the right of the Creator alone to enter into, go out of, and evoke movements in a person's spirit, drawing it whole into love of the Divine Majesty. I say "without cause," meaning without any foregoing perception or awareness of an object from which — through the workings of the person's understanding and will — such a consolation might come.

Third Norm. When there is some cause present, either a good [331] angel or an evil spirit can be consoling a person, but for different purposes. The good angel consoles for a person's progress, that he may grow and advance from good to better. The evil spirit consoles for the opposite of that and so that eventually he can draw a person into his accursed design and wickedness.

Fourth Norm. It is characteristic of an evil spirit to mask as an [332] angel of light. He starts out supporting the deeply committed person and ends recruiting him. As an instance, he comes with good and holy thoughts familiar to committed people but then, a step at a time, he manages to leave that way and to draw the person into his hidden fallacies and perverse design.

Fifth Norm. We need, then, to watch carefully the whole trend [333] of our thoughts. If in the beginning, middle, and end they are all good and lead only to good, that marks them as coming from the good angel. But the trend of thoughts from a spirit can end in something bad or distracting; or it can end in a lesser good than the committed person had earlier planned; or weaken, upset, or disturb him, thieving the peace, tranquility, and quiet he had had before. That trend signals clearly that the thoughts come from an evil spirit, an enemy of our spiritual growth and eternal salvation.

Sixth Norm. Once the enemy of our humankind has been de- [334] tected and recognized by his serpent's tail and by the bad end he leads to, the person he tempted will do well to look at the whole trend of his thoughts. He would trace the good thoughts suggested to him back to their beginning; then look at how the evil spirit managed one step at a time to make him fall away from the sweet spiritual joy he had had and finally drew him to his own corrupt purpose. He does this so that, once he has grasped his experience and learned from it, he can defend himself in the future against the enemy's usual deceits.

Seventh Norm. Persons making progress and going from good [335] to better, the good angel touches gently, lightly, and sweetly, like a drop of water falling into a sponge. The evil spirit touches them smartly, with noise and commotion, like a drop of water falling on a stone.

Persons going from bad to worse, the spirits touch in reversed ways.

The reason for this lies in the person's spiritual condition, which will be either contrary to a given spirit or harmonious with it. So when a person's spiritual condition opposes a spirit, the spirit comes in with noise and notable commotion; but when his condition is harmonious with a given spirit, it comes in quietly, as through an open door into its own home.

[336]     Eighth Norm. As has been said, consolation without previous cause comes only from God our Lord and hence has nothing of deception in it. However, the spiritual person to whom God grants this consolation does well to consider it very alertly, cautiously distinguishing the actual period of the consolation itself from the period following it, during which the person continues fervent and favored with the graces and with the lingering effects of the consolation now passed.

The reason is that commonly enough during this second period a person forms various plans and proposals that are not given immediately by God our Lord. He might be moved by his habits, persuaded by his own reasoning, drawn by the logic of his own judgments. He might be moved by a good spirit. Or an evil spirit. Consequently, he has to inspect these plans and proposals very carefully before giving them full credit or enacting them.

## ✛ Comment 22 ✛

# Leaving the Exercises

As you can now appreciate, the Spiritual Exercises invite you to make great choices and to change the way you see the world. They open you to the Holy Spirit's teaching, which means that you can find God in all things, not as nirvana or an escape, but as the Holy One working busily within the world and inviting you to work too.

If you can maintain this awareness, which you will manage only if you do justice and walk humbly with God in the church, you will live as a contemplative in action. You will, finally, find yourself continually called to wonder, What more can I do to fill up the work of our Lord and Master Jesus Christ?

# Chronology

1491    Ignatius is born, baptized Iñigo López de Loyola.

1506    Iñigo goes for training to the court of Juan Velázquez de Cuéllar.

1517    He joins the entourage of the Viceroy of Navarre as *gentilhombre*.

1521    Iñigo gravely wounded at Pamplona and carried to Loyola. Surgeries on his knee; he nearly dies. He reads a life of Jesus Christ and lives of the saints. A profound conversion.

1522    At Montserrat, he makes his confession. A pilgrim-beggar, he lives penitentially for a year at Manresa. The great illumination by the River Cardoner.

1523    Iñigo leaves Manresa carrying the first writings of *Spiritual Exercises*. He pauses in Barcelona and then goes to the Holy Land.

1524    Unable to remain in the Holy Land, he returns through Venice to Barcelona.

1525    In Barcelona, he studies Latin with boys, preparing to study theology. He continues giving Spiritual Exercises.

1526    In Alcalá, Iñigo begins studies, is imprisoned and tried by the Inquisition.

1527    In Salamanca, he studies briefly. He turns over his handwritten *Spiritual Exercises* to the Inquisition. His freedom to give spiritual counsel is curtailed.

1528    He goes to Paris, to the College of Montaigu, signing himself Ignatius of Loyola. He continues giving Spiritual Exercises and writes "Principle and Foundation," "Three Sorts of People," and "Three Models of Humility."

1529    He enrolls at the College of Sainte Barbe, rooming with Francis Xavier and Pierre Favre.

1532    Ignatius of Loyola is granted the Bachelor of Arts.

1534     He is made Master of Arts. Ignatius takes the first six Companions through Spiritual Exercises. On August 15, at Montmartre, all vow to lead an evangelical life.

1535     Leaving the Companions in Paris, Ignatius spends time in Spain and then goes to Venice, to work in poor houses and give Exercises.

1537     In January, the Companions reunite in Venice and spend a year trying to get to Jerusalem. Ignatius and others ordained priests. They all give Spiritual Exercises. Ignatius writes out "The Mysteries of the Life of Christ Our Lord" and "Norms about Good Order in Eating for the Future."

1538     In Rome and environs, they continue giving Exercises. They are accused of heterodoxy and go through a court trial.

1539     The Companions ask to form a new religious order; Pope Paul III gives verbal approval. Ignatius composes "Norms for Thinking within the Church."

1540     Papal bull *Regimini militantis ecclesiae* establishes the Company of Jesus. Ignatius completes the major Norms of his book's appendix. Francis Xavier leaves for India.

1541     Ignatius unanimously elected general.

1544     Ignatius prepares the autograph copy of *Spiritual Exercises*. He begins composing the *Constitutions of the Company of Jesus*. The Company quickly grows in number.

1548     *Spiritual Exercises* formally approved by Paul III and printed. Ignatius leads the Company into the work of education, establishing at Messina the first Jesuit college.

1550     The first draft of the *Constitutions* is ready for examination by the founding members.

1551     With the pope's approval, Ignatius establishes the Roman College and continues opening other colleges.

1556     On 31 July, Ignatius of Loyola dies.

# Bibliography

Ignatius of Loyola. *The Autobiography of St. Ignatius Loyola*. Trans. Joseph F. O'Callaghan; ed. with introduction and notes by John C. Olin. New York: Harper & Row, 1974. This is the story of his life dictated to a younger Companion. The Introduction and notes clarify a good deal.

————. *Letters of St. Ignatius of Loyola*. Trans. William J. Young, S.J. Chicago: Loyola University Press, 1959. The fullest collection in English from Ignatius of Loyola's seven thousand extant letters, many dealing with spiritual direction.

————. *Ignatius of Loyola The Spiritual Exercises and Selected Works*. Ed. George E. Ganss, S.J. New York: Paulist Press, 1991. The editor provides a long introduction and excellent footnoting to his own scholarly translation of *Spiritual Exercises* and to translations by several experts of Ignatius's *Autobiography*, *Spiritual Diary*, selected parts of the *Constitutions*, and a number of letters. The best collection of texts in English.

————. *The Spiritual Exercises of Saint Ignatius of Loyola Translated from the Spanish with a Commentary and a Translation of the Directorium in Exercitia*. 5th ed. Trans. W. H. Longridge. London: A. R. Mowbray, 1955. The author makes spiritual and ascetical comments on each sentence of the text. His translation of the *Directory* of 1599 is the only one currently available in English.

————. *The Spiritual Exercises: A Literal Translation and a Contemporary Reading*. Trans. Elder Mullan, S.J., and David Fleming, S.J., 1980. Reprint. St. Louis: Institute of Jesuit Sources, 1989. The translation was made in 1914 and is tightly literal; the contemporary reading is a paraphrase. The two are juxtaposed page by page.

————. *The Spiritual Exercises of St. Ignatius Loyola*. Trans. Elisabeth M. Tetlow. Lanham, Md.: University Press of America, 1987. This translation successfully avoids all sexist language.

Bangert, William V., S.J. *A History of the Society of Jesus*. St. Louis: Institute of Jesuit Sources, 1972. The most available general history of the Jesuits.

Clancy, Thomas H., S.J. *The Conversational Word of God*. St. Louis: Institute of Jesuit Sources, 1978. The author translates four early Jesuit texts on conversation as an apostolate and explores Ignatius's creativity in an activity closely related to the *Spiritual Exercises*.

Cusson, Gilles, S.J. *Biblical Theology and the Spiritual Exercises*. Trans. Mary A. Roduit, R.C., and George E. Ganss, S.J. St. Louis: Institute of Jesuit Sources, 1988. The most thorough theological commentary presently available in English and one of the finest in any language. Based on both scholarship and years of experience.

Dalmases, Cándido de, S.J. *Ignatius of Loyola, Founder of the Jesuits: His Life and Work*. Trans. Jerome Aixalá. St. Louis: Institute of Jesuit Sources, 1985. The most recent popular life of the author, based on current scholarship.

Egan, Harvey D., S.J. *Ignatius Loyola the Mystic*. Wilmington, Del.: Michael Glazier, 1987. The book draws a fine portrait of Ignatius as a man while underscoring both his profound mysticism and the practicality of his *Spiritual Exercises*.

Guibert, Joseph de, S.J. *The Jesuits: The Spiritual Doctrine and Practice*. Trans. William J. Young. Chicago: Loyola University Press, 1964; St. Louis: Institute of Jesuit Sources, 1986. This historical and thematic study of Jesuit spirituality is currently without peer; the author covers the origin, dynamic, and the practice of the *Spiritual Exercises*.

Rahner, Hugo, S.J. *Ignatius the Theologian*. Trans. Michael Barry, S.J. New York: Herder and Herder, 1968. A relatively early and excellent synthesis of Ignatius's spiritual theology.

Rahner, Karl, S.J. *Spiritual Exercises*. Trans. Kenneth Baker, S.J. New York: Herder and Herder, 1965. The text of the talks preached by a preeminent theologian as an eight-day retreat to younger Jesuits.

Ravier, André, S.J. *Ignatius of Loyola and the Founding of the Society of Jesus*. San Francisco: Ignatius Press, 1988. A biography of Ignatius of Loyola focusing on his life as the founder of the Company of Jesus.

Tetlow, Joseph A., S.J. *Choosing Christ in the World*. St. Louis: Institute of Jesuit Sources, 1989. This handbook gives materials and instructions for directing the Spiritual Exercises at home.

van Breemen, Peter, S.J. *As Bread That Is Broken*. Denville, N.J.: Dimension Books, 1987. A current and very successful instance of a spiritual book based directly on the materials of the *Spiritual Exercises*.